The Confusion Experiment

*A 100 day journey from the head
to the heart and beyond*

by

Camille Conte

Christy Morgan — Literary Mentor & Editor
Emil Churchin — Assistant Editor
Proofreader — Peggy Beal
Janet Levin — Creative Consultant
Corinna Delgado & Nadina Simon — Cover Design
Dan Granda — Book Layout

ISBN-13: 978-1722842093
ISBN-10: 1722842091

Mark!

I'm delighted our paths remain crossed. Thank you for all of your support.

Enjoy the ride! May my journey inspire your own

Peace Camille

Foreword

A year and a half ago, I was honored to meet Camille Conte. She came to work with me as a client to find a voice, to face her fears, and to learn as much about herself as possible. When I first met her, I noticed that she was nervous and anxious, maybe a bit scared, but was wide open. She had no idea what we were going to do, but that didn't stop her from being willing to go deep and open up to the unknown.

After working with thousands and thousands of people, I have to say Camille's commitment to change is remarkable. She's been completely dedicated to her own growth. I remember at one point, her continually telling me, "I don't understand? I'm so confused." I suggested that she should write and talk about that confusion. She would then become even more confused and reply, "So you're saying that my 'voice' is to be confused? That's my ticket??" Yes—we have to let this confusion happen and not seek to find an answer right away, so that we can become a space for a higher calling to come through. I challenged her to meditate for 100 days and make a video immediately afterwards exploring the experience. I was shocked to learn that she had done it. Every single day, this woman committed to going inward, listening in deep meditation, and creating a daily video series—all while writing a book and transforming as a human being.

To me, the only people that I want to listen to are people who have actually experienced change, versus just studying how it works. Camille has experienced change, she became change, and she embodied change. Many of the old habits that she had lingering around seem to have vanished. She now is embodying a unique voice and confidence that offers us an incredible opportunity to question our own fears, to fall in love with our confusion, and to create a space for a much more powerful us. This is the version of ourselves that could actually make a major change, not only for our lives and the people around us, but for the entire planet.

There is no question that Camille has done the work so deeply that she has transcended many of the challenges that she grew up with in her past. Every one of us has some sort of lingering belief system that we could look at and move beyond. There are many people that could tell us "how" to look at it, but there are very few that actually do the work. Camille actually looked at it, loved it, faced it, and stayed with it until Life, the Universe, or whatever else you want to call it, took it from her. In this book, Camille lives a transformation for us. She experiences her fears, the excitement, and the possibilities, and then proves her new confident embodiment by living it—and that's why Camille is a gift. It feels to me like maybe 16 people on the planet have actually done that type of work. Camille is one of them.

I know there are so many people who are experts in many different fields, but I'd rather learn skydiving from someone who skydives than from someone who has only studied skydiving. Camille was so courageous that she walked right into the heart of a very well-developed limitation and stayed with it until it was gone. To me, that is what a hero does. She is my hero, and I'm honored to be a part of her book because she is living the real truth.

-Kyle Cease

Comedian, Speaker and Author of *New York Times* Bestseller, *I Hope I Screw This Up*

Acknowledgements

I wouldn't be writing my first ever acknowledgments page if Kyle Cease hadn't challenged me to write about my confusion, with the added motivation of "I'll write it if you don't." Kyle was convinced, "There's a book here," and he was right.

There wouldn't be any words if Christy Morgan hadn't said "Yes" to my Facebook post looking for someone to transcribe the one hundred videos. That she had attended many of my workshops in Alaska years before added a layer of destiny to this moment. I didn't know then that Christy is a phenomenal editor and talented writer herself. Transcribing the videos allowed Christy to wear my skin, which became a priceless gift as we moved forward because she understood intrinsically what I had gone through and what I was trying to convey. Christy single-handedly showed me my voice, kept me true to it, and – through her edits – made it more powerful. She helped me let go of what I was clinging to, taught me about writing and editing in a way that shaped this work, and fought for my authenticity even when I was willing to surrender it. In the home stretch, she went back in for the fourth and then fifth edit of the 100 days, doing for me what I couldn't do myself, which was to shave away everything that wasn't necessary. In turn, we created exactly what I had always wanted. Christy has put hundreds of hours into this project, very little of which was compensated. I would not have this book without you, Christy and I am forever grateful.

I wouldn't have been able to pay Christy for that initial transcription work if it weren't for the following people who donated to my first ever "Book Shower", a fun spoof on having a baby shower (as this certainly is my baby). Thank you Kay Howard, John Stabb, Laurel Epps, Mary Kay and Terry Welsh, Cynthia Hensley, Evie Dunham, Karen Button, Dawn Kelly, Bud Jahn, Meghan Piersma, Ron Swartz, Mark Anthony, Susan Brakeall and Mark Pearson. Thank you so much for being the first ones to buy the book!

I wouldn't have said, "Yes" to the Flow Group retreat if it weren't for my beautiful mentor, Shirley Mae Springer Staten, who made it so very clear and easy when she said, "Tell them you're in!" I don't know that I would have taken the book seriously if Shirley hadn't gotten up from her couch, after I returned from the Flow Group weekend, with a piece of white paper and insisted I fold it in half and write across the top, "The Confusion Experiment." I think back now at how annoyed I was that she was forcing me to do something so stupid. Thank you, Shirley, for seeing the cover before I could.

I wouldn't have been able to make that weekend in California happen on such short notice if it weren't for my dear friend, Vicki Watson, who became an Angel investor in January of 2017, long before any of this was in the works. Vicki donated to my radio show's annual fundraiser, and the amount was so considerable that I immediately knew this was seed money for something special, although at the time I didn't know what. I held onto that check until March 17th, when I used it in a way that snowballed into one financial miracle after another that paid for the weekend's expenses. I wouldn't have been able to afford the weekend's lodging if it weren't for my beloved soul sister, Christina Young, who wrote me a check to pay for it without hesitation. And I wouldn't have had any extra spending money if it weren't for my long-time friend and radio brother, Cary

Carrigan and his wife Lynn, who gifted me with some beautiful green cash just hours before I left.

I wouldn't have had the feedback that further crafted the book without my three groups of readers who agreed to a short turn-around and gave constructive criticism that made the book better each time. Additional thanks to Mary Hasbrouck, Claire Coppel, Patty Bran, Katie Povolo, Kim Wilson, and Colinda Wolfe for their feedback and insight.

I wouldn't have been able to begin the process of getting myself ready to do the edits that had to be done if it weren't for Emil Churchin, a dear friend and talented writer. Emil was one of my first readers who asked me to let him "clean up the punctuation." A few days later, he made a very strong case to let him have editing rights. Realizing it would be good to have a fresh set of eyes, Christy and I said yes. As Emil combed through the pages in Google docs, I began to hyperventilate as one yellow comment box after another crowded the right side of the page. Long, thoughtful reasoning as to why I needed to edit this and cut that left me defensive. Christy, knowing he was right and understanding my resistance, was able to help me see the light, patiently walking me through each and every edit. Emil's deep dedication to my writing, his devotion to our friendship and me "getting this right," his relentless unwilling-ness to go easy on me, his brilliant insight into what the reader would tolerate and question, his gentle exasperation of my ob-session with the word, "profound," and his loving support of me being an author ("Stop saying you're not an author! I'm edit-ing your book!"), created a turning point in what the book was able to become. Emil, too, spent over a hundred hours editing and received a tiny stipend for work that is priceless.

Unending gratitude to my prayer partner and soul brother, Kaleem Nuriddin. Through his undying dedication to my high-est good, he has held a space for me every Wednesday morning for the past four years. He knew and affirmed with me what was coming before it took form and felt the impact the book would make on people's lives for months leading up to the publication.

My thanks to Sarah for her support over that retreat weekend and to Kara, for holding such a space of love for all of us as we journeyed to the depths of our souls. I'm grateful for our friendship.

I wouldn't have been able to go so deep inside myself that weekend if it weren't for Mark, Kat and Sacha, three remarkably brave individuals whose lives and choices have inspired me beyond measure. To you, Sacha, there are few words I've left unsaid to describe how much I love you and how your presence in my life since March 23, 2017 has forever changed the quality of my existence. How true it is, my friend, that butterflies are free.

Lastly, deep appreciation to my sisters Judy and Janice for their continuous support and encouragement. Nothing but love for my tremendous mother, Ann, The World's Greatest Joke Teller, who was willing to let me write about her, her experience of aging and our experience as mother and daughter. My mom remains my #1 cheerleader and has always believed in me. She will be forever remembered for her most often spoken five words, "I'm so proud of you!"

This is for you, Mom.

Peace Camille

Introduction

Welcome to The Confusion Experiment, my 100 days of meditation and documentation. For the record, I'm not here to teach you how to meditate. I'm here to share the twists and turns, the ups and downs of the literal and metaphorical trip I took into myself, through myself, and back out into the world. In telling this story, I am hoping to connect with you and with other people who have had similar experiences. I want to be part of a caravan of adventurers who are willing to go inward and blow the roof off of how they show up in life.

Before we take the journey to the center of my mind, I want to give you some insight to the layout of this book. In part one, I tell you about what led to my life-altering weekend in March of 2017 with Kyle Cease, the Transformation Comedian and New York Times Best-Selling Author, as well as the weekend itself. That's when I accepted the challenge that became The Confusion Experiment: to meditate one hour a day for one hundred days, to roll a video after each meditation describing the experience, and then post it on Facebook. Kyle also challenged me to write about my confusion, telling me, "There's a book here." At the time I didn't believe him, but here it is. Part two, "The 100 Days", is the experiment itself, where I used meditation to heal my confusion. In part three, "Journey to the Center of the Mind," I offer the experiment's findings and some final thoughts.

Much of my writing leading to Day One of my experiment is stream of consciousness that jets ahead and then goes back in time. It's a mirror of what was going on inside of me, and my fingers got the dictation job. In order to honor my confusion and what was happening, I have chosen to let it run its course. I hope you'll stay with me, as I learned to stay with myself, through one of the most extraordinary adventures of a lifetime: the transformation of the self.

Chapter 1

Be Careful What You Ask For

This story begins...well, I can't really put a pin in where it begins, but for now I'm starting with January 1, 2017. I came into the new year with a very clear intention: to help 10,000 people take the inward journey, to come home to their real Self and set it free. Though I wondered how the hell I was going to reach that many people and why it had to be ten thousand, I decided it was time to stretch myself into the vision I felt was calling me so ten thousand it was. And with that, the new year began with me wanting to assist people experience personal transformation. What I didn't realize then, of course, was that to do so I had to first go through my own.

I also started 2017 in New Jersey, helping my mom. Since 2014, I've been traveling back and forth from Alaska to spend more time with her as she climbs into her eighties, and to serve her as her needs change. She still lives in the same house I grew up in, so when I'm back in New Jersey I live in my small childhood bedroom, complete with the psychedelic floral wallpaper I enjoyed so much more when I was sixteen. It's here, in this room, where, as a child, I dreamed my life's dream of being a famous New York radio disc jockey. As a kid, I was mesmerized by the voices that came through my small transistor radio, with its wrist strap that let me take it wherever I went. At night, I tucked it under my pillow and drifted off to sleep with some of the great jocks of all time talking directly to me. It was magic, and I wanted to be the magician. Later, in my teens, as FM radio took hold and the album rock format made its entrance, I remained spellbound by the women who worked at New York's WNEW FM: Allison Steele, Meg Griffin and Carol Miller. This bedroom held so many dreams. It made total sense that I was in New Jersey for much of this transformation. I was tilling the very soil that got me here.

The new year rolled into February. I had been in Jersey for four months by that point, continuing to deal with the one thing that hadn't changed in three years of living on and off with my mother and becoming her caregiver: I wasn't putting the oxygen mask on myself first, and my tank was empty. There's a reason why they warn against that on planes. You're of no use to yourself, let alone anyone else, if you can't breathe. Suffice to say, things were not going well for me. My stress level was rising as I attempted to further my life's purpose with aggressive focus while also tending to my mom, a nearly impossible combination at the time. I needed a break. If you've ever been an adult caregiver yourself, you know exactly what I'm talking about.

In fact, while writing this story, an article in AARP confirmed my reality. "Family caregivers in New Jersey provided more than 1 billion hours of care — worth an estimated $13.6 billion — to their parents, spouses, partners, and other adult loved ones in 2015." I used to think caregiving meant that someone was near death, but my experience has humbled me into an understanding that caregiving begins much sooner than that and takes on many shapes and duties. In my mom's case, it started with helping out with her bills after my dad died in 2008, then doing her taxes and other administrative tasks, and quickly moved into managing and repairing her 1960s home. When we made the tough decision to take away her car keys, the roles of daughter and mother began to blur as I drove her to and from appointments, and my caregiving duties went up a notch. I witnessed firsthand the grief my mom experienced at the loss of her driving privilege and it caused me tremendous emotional pain to take that independence away from her. One day I didn't know where she was; looking from the kitchen window I saw her sitting in her car in the driver's seat, her hands on the wheel and the door ajar, wearing a look I'll never forget. Her face showed longing, nostalgia and resignation that this part of her life was over. My tears fell hard onto the sink's shiny surface. This, coupled with the inevitable loss of her beloved friends, put me in the front row of my mom's aging process, a show I didn't like seeing but had to bear witness to, though I sometimes squirmed in my seat while doing so.

And still, my mom remains quite vibrant in many areas of her life. For those who listen to my podcast, The Camille Conte Show, you know my mom as The World's Greatest Joke Teller, who can drop a punchline like no one else. But after living on my own in Alaska for 30 years, I simply wasn't prepared for what I had taken on as a caregiver. Truth is, I didn't know I had taken it on. It crept up on me, task by task, and by the time I realized what was happening it was too late. I missed my friends and my life as I knew it, and I was struggling to make ends meet. Though I was doing all I could to generate an income, I was sliding downhill. I was spending most of the time trying to create products from the courses and workshops I taught in Alaska to feature on my new spiritual education website. It was taking longer than I had thought.

There's more to say about this experience and I do so in the 100 Days but for now, I had yet to learn how to manage the situation, and I created a lot of stress for myself and for my mom as well. It didn't help that I believed I was failing miserably at my goal of reorganizing my career path, which was producing a damaging level of stress I wasn't fully aware of until I got into The Confusion Experiment.

I knew I needed a break and kept getting the nudge to go somewhere and relax. My heart leapt up and said, *Let's go to Hawaii! You said you wanted to go to Maui, let's do that.* I called my friend Curtis, who lives in Maui, and he kindly offered the use of his man cave and his car. I took it as a sign that this was meant to be. So I went online to check airfares. While combing through prices, a very familiar feeling began to trickle into my body and a very familiar story started to come into my mind...You can't do this, you can't afford it. You're not working a full-time job. You can't - you can't - what if - what if?

This has happened before: this voice, the voice of my mind, squashing what I know in my heart and how I want to live my life. By the end of the night I was sitting on the edge of my old, squeaky trundle bed feeling sad and depressed. I actually said out loud, "Wow, you've pretty much talked yourself out of this, haven't you?" It took a long time to fall asleep that night.

The next day I was browsing Facebook and randomly saw an ad. The phrase, "The Transformational Comedian" caught my attention. I found that interesting, so I clicked on it and there was Kyle Cease, a former Comedy Central comedian, talking about personal growth. I watched his video and had an immediate resonance with it. This led me to his website, where there were plenty of other videos. The next one to catch my eye was called, "Your Money is Worth What You Spend It On." *Hmm*, I thought, *let's see what this is going to say*.

Seconds in, I realized that the video was describing what I had just experienced the day before when I was arguing with myself about being able to afford a vacation. Kyle said the greatest investment we can ever make with our money is in our own self growth. Watching his video helped me understand what had happened and why it happened, and I vowed never to let it happen again. If my heart wanted to go to Hawaii, my mind was just going to have to get on board or I'd leave without it.

But the next day there was something about going to Maui that just wasn't there anymore. The urgency to go to that specific place had tapered off. I thought it was odd, but I decided to trust the feeling and not force it. I knew I still needed a break, though, and felt like I had gotten permission to invest in my well-being and I believed something would make sense. In a flash, I remembered that I'd seen an advertisement for a meditation retreat over Memorial Day weekend with Dr. Michael Beckwith, the spiritual leader at Agape International Spiritual Center in California. Suddenly, that was feeling right to my heart. I called the Center for details and realized I had just enough money on my credit card to pay for the registration. Instead of securing my spot right then and there I told the gentleman on the phone, "Let me check the airfares and I'll get back to you." I hung up, unaware of my pattern of sabotage, and went downstairs to cook dinner for my mom. As I was chopping garlic I heard myself saying, "Let me go check airfares..." I gasped, dropped the knife onto the counter and ran back up the steps thinking to myself, *Hell no. I'm not doing that again!*

I immediately called the Agape Center back and registered for the weekend. When I hung up the phone I felt really good, like I had defeated a monster. In three months, I'd be going to a meditation retreat, something I've always wanted to do. I'd been meditating for about ten years in varying degrees of commitment and was ready to up my game. This would be perfect. Plus the feeling I had about going was really exciting, exactly how I'd felt a few days prior thinking about Maui. Though the meditation retreat was still three months away, I decided to believe that all was as it should be and it would work out.

Later that night, I went back to Kyle's website and watched more of his videos. He was echoing exactly what I had been thinking about, talking about, and going through these last several months. Two days later, I finished binge-watching every single one of them. Then I saw something titled, "Flow Group". I clicked to watch. "If you've gotten this far," Kyle said, "that means you want more."

In this video, he talked about his very intimate coaching experience with four people selected to spend the weekend together in California. Now that got my attention. I had been wanting support like this since 2012, when I began to rearrange my career as a rock 'n roll radio broadcaster to combine my passion for spiritual education with my love for music. At the time, I knew something was calling me. I didn't know what it was, but I could feel it coming from a very deep place within me - which is why, in October of 2013, I actually took a leap of faith to answer that call and jabbed a stick in the wheel of my life, hoping that stopping it long enough would allow for something fresh to begin. (More on that later.)

Clarity was something I had definitely been seeking since that time because though I began a process of identifying my skills and talents to transfer them to something new, I wasn't quite sure where I was going. As I did this throughout 2014, 2015, and 2016, I felt like I needed someone to help guide me and I believed Kyle Cease was the person I had been looking for. I watched as Kyle explained that, to be considered for the weekend, you had to record a video telling him why you should be picked. Well, I knew exactly why I was the perfect person for this weekend. "I'm doing it," I said out loud, and I closed my laptop feeling happier than I had in quite some time.

The next day, I printed out the questions that the website offered as a guide, and I made my video downstairs on my mother's porch on a sunny, warm February afternoon. I hadn't realized how emotional I was feeling about my life and all that I'd been trying to accomplish until I recorded that video. Watching myself pour my heart out with such passion was an overwhelming experience. I was in awe of what I was saying. Was this really inside me all this time? I talked about a world that could work for everyone, how I wanted to help people live their best life, how I wanted to be a part of the solution, and how I just needed somebody to mentor me there. Creating my submission video allowed me to powerfully articulate my certainty about two things: I wanted to live from my heart all the time, and I was ready to see what other gifts I might have waiting within me.

I had no idea that I had just given a command to the Universe. At the end of my viewing, something suddenly came through me. Everything tingled. I had a short but complete flash of insight that brought the hair up on my entire body. I was lit up for at least 10 seconds as this multi-media preview flowed through me. *Kyle's assistants are going to watch this video and they're going to tell him to watch this video, and after he does he'll tell them to call me up and get me in the next Flow Group.* This vision was as real as any moment we call real. I was so fired up, so damn excited, as I watched the video another 10 or 12 times. I couldn't get enough of it!! I knew this was going to happen because I know when I know something, and I KNEW this.

I sent the video off the next day and spent the rest of the week preparing to leave for Anchorage. It's never easy to say goodbye to my mom. She's been gracious letting me come and go so that it's win/win for both of us, but she doesn't ever want me to leave. Italian mothers like their daughters nearby! I left New Jersey on February 28th, arriving in Alaska to the tune of 6 degrees below zero. I forgot about my video application, though not about my mom; caregiving never leaves the caregiver.

Chapter 2

The Last Frontier

One main reason I returned to Alaska was to co-host an event with my beloved friend, Shirley Mae. We had a women's retreat scheduled on March 24th, 25th, and 26th in Big Lake, Alaska; however, we hadn't gotten anyone to sign up yet and there was less than a month to go. Shirley and I hosted this women's weekend once before, in the fall of 2016, and we had seen a tremendous response that led to a short waiting list of women interested in attending this next one. I was stumped as to why we hadn't had any bites yet. Meanwhile, Kurt, the owner of the house, was asking for a deposit to hold the dates. We requested three more days so we could figure out what was going on. He graciously agreed.

There was much to be done in three days if we were going to secure enough participants to make this a go. Then, on the afternoon of March 13, I went to my computer and there was an email from Kara, Kyle Cease's assistant. My heart stopped. The memory of my certainty flooded back in. I knew it! I knew it!! I knew it!!!

Hi Camille!

We are so excited to watch your video. I used the link below but it tells me that the video is not available.

Sincerely,

Kara

What?! How can that be? I went to YouTube, fixed the problem, re-sent the video and was relieved when Kara confirmed being able to view it. I waited. Nothing. I waited some more. Nothing. A nail biter - and since I've never had long nails, it was a short trip. It was late afternoon, and I could hardly contain myself. I decided I needed to go somewhere to distract myself. I headed out to watch a movie, hoping to get lost in another world. I barely managed to do that. When I got back home, I rushed to my laptop and checked my email. It was now 9:00 pm and I saw that the following message had been waiting for me since 6:00 pm.

Hello Lovely Flow Group Submitters!

First thank you so much for your videos :) It has been our pleasure to watch them. For those of you who we've had trouble opening your video links you've already been reached out to in a separate email.

This email is to let you know that we've had a recent opening for our March 24th-26th Flow Group! Yay! This is a major double yay because this is potentially our last Flow Group of the year. With Kyle's book being released in May, our schedule has become quite full. We've had so many submissions and thus are inquiring, if selected, would you be able to attend the March Flow Group? The weekend starts mid-day Friday, the 24th, with full days on Saturday and Sunday.

If this is a big yes for you please let me know as you all are specifically wonderful so most likely we will work on a first come first serve basis.

Sincerely,

Kara

Flow Group Coordinator

Oh my gosh, oh my gosh! This was incredible. The currency of life itself was flowing through me with such power in that moment. I was lost in an "out of this world" feeling beyond description. And then, with a sudden drop in my heart, I realized the Flow Group retreat with Kyle was on the same weekend Shirley and I were scheduled to lead our own retreat. WTF?!

I called Shirley right away and told her the whole story in one breath, asking, "What should I do?" With all the unconditional love that is within her, she calmly said, "Tell Kara you're in."

"Really?" My heart was pounding. "How would you feel if we cancel the retreat?" I asked.

"Relieved," she said, laughing. "Our retreat is eleven days away and we've got no one signed up." And then it dawned on both of us: this must be why nobody registered for our event! I wasn't going to be here for it; I was going to be in California! The lack of response and attendees, so perplexing before, was now evidence of incredible synchronicity. Right then and there, I replied to Kara's email and wrote, "I'm in."

I hung up the phone with Shirley, only to call her back fifteen minutes later. I was so overwhelmed by what was happening that my mind was spinning and my heart was leaping. I needed to talk more about this amazing turn of events so that the reality of the situation could sink into them both.

By this point it was nearly 11:00 pm, and Shirley and I had ended what turned out to be another hour of highly charged conversation. I made myself a cup of tea and put another log in the fireplace, a warm and wonderful glow, the only thing lighting the darkened room. As I sat there, staring into the flames, something extraordinary happened. A mystical experience began to descend upon me. Suddenly I heard the sounds of a cocktail party with faint music in the background, glasses clinking, the fabulous chatter of a crowd of people swarming over each other with stories and laughter. The accompanying feeling was one of joy and celebration. And then I heard Its voice, a voice that held within It all the voices of those who love me, all my guardian angels and spirit guides, with even my father's distinctive tone layered in. "This is for you." the Voice of voices said. "We're so excited for you!" I closed my eyes and joined them in the celebration that would last long into the night.

The next morning, Tuesday, I got an email from Kara letting me know that Kyle wanted to see my video. I cannot even begin to describe what I felt. Do you ever get that feeling about something, where you know what's going to happen even though there isn't any evidence to prove that you could know what you know? That's what I experienced.

I sent the video link, and what do you know? Kyle couldn't watch that video either! So I corrected it again and off it went. I spent the day telling myself to relax but that wasn't possible. I was checking my email every hour and nothing. There was no response all day and all night long. My mind was working overtime. How could they not communicate something?! By the end of the night I was exhausted but somehow managed to keep my spirits high remembering that I already knew how this was going to turn out.

The next day, Wednesday, I was on the phone with my beloved prayer partner, Kaleem. It was 6:00 am and 10 below zero. The morning sky was like night, with Venus hanging right outside the window and the promise of a world beyond. It was a wonderful opportunity to share the story with yet another friend who has been a part of my life for twenty years. We prayed a prayer of knowing the Truth and the perfection of this entire experience. After I hung up, I fell back to sleep.

I awoke hours later and before my eyes were open, my mind said, "Check the airfares to Los Angeles." As if there were a person in the room, I replied, "Hell no! I'm definitely not doing that, that's for sure.

Buoyed by the spiritual exchange with Kaleem, Wednesday morning was a continuation of the mystical experience that I was going through. I was in a heightened state of awareness as I waited to hear back from Kara. The Presence was all around me. It was palpable. For all these years in which I have been reaching out and then inward, seeking It through my practices, It was with me that day in a way that was beyond anything I had ever known before. I felt so supported, so loved. I could hear It whispering in my ear and I listened; I listened deeply.

At 1:00 pm I got the email from Kara I had been waiting for:

Hi Camille,

Do you have time to chat around 2:30 pm-3:00 pm PST today?

I sat and looked at that email for what seemed like eternity. It felt like electricity was lighting up my nervous system. I responded to her with my phone number, and then the call came in.

"Hi Camille, it's Kara."

"Yes, I know. Hi Kara."

"Camille, Kyle wants you to know that you're the winner."

I burst into tears. I was jumping up and down and screaming. Then I told her everything that happened in less than half a breath. I had to let her know that I knew she was in the story before she knew I was in the Flow Group! And she was blown away by that.

Now it was time to take care of the logistics. I had said yes to this experience without knowing how it was all going to come together, which is code for how I was going to pay for it. Airfare, money for the Airbnb, and of course the chunk of change the weekend itself would cost - these were all things I had to figure out. Turns out, it was already done for me. One miracle after another showed up. One came in the form of an increased credit card limit the very day I was selected for the exact amount of the registration cost. Seriously. Financial gifts came from dear friends who were so thrilled for me that they wanted to help make this happen. Everything lined up better than I could have ever put it together. It was further proof of the power of active faith, the power of believing, the power of getting out of the way and letting the Intelligence that holds the planets in place handle things far better than anything my limited mind could have orchestrated. When I finally did check airfares, I found two one-way flights for less than $150 each. It was a 24-hour whirlwind with thousands of dollars flowing through my hands. Meanwhile, Shirley and I canceled the women's retreat, and the next thing I knew I was flying to Los Angeles, staying in a million-dollar house, and watching Kyle Cease pull up in the driveway.

One other thing you should know. Right before I left Alaska for the Flow Group retreat in Los Angeles, I told a few close friends and my family what I felt was going to happen that weekend with Kyle. I knew I was going to get answers and have clarity. I was going to get direction. I was going to come home with the information I believed that I didn't have, and I was going to move my life forward. My calendar was going to be full of activity, money was going to flow in and build, Shirley and I were going to have sold out events... this was going to happen and that was going to happen, and I was so excited. It was the break I'd been looking for!

By the end of the retreat's first night, I knew I was screwed.

Chapter 3

This Is Not What I Ordered

Our Flow Group of four included my fellow travelers for the weekend: Kat, Mark, and Sacha. Kat lived in the area and didn't stay in the house with us, so Sacha, Mark and I spent the most time together. Sacha was from Australia. Mark from Rochester, New York.

I landed in L.A. the day before the retreat. Sacha had gotten there early as well, and I was excited about meeting another attendee before we started the weekend. I met Sacha at the Denny's near LAX and knew her as soon as I walked in. The first thing I saw was the flower tucked behind her right ear adorning her wavy brown hair that fell just past her shoulders. *So feminine*, I thought as I approached the table. I wished I had the confidence to wear one too, suddenly yearning for my own expression of softness. My first hours with Sacha felt like two best friends who hadn't seen each other in a while but had no problem dropping deep down into the heart of the matter. We were immediately speaking to each other with a depth of honesty and authenticity that lit me up. Our connection felt like it had already been coordinated in the soup of the Universe. I sat in Denny's in utter awe, licking the salt off my fingers that the crispy French fries had left behind, as she told me her story, punctuated with exclamations of amazement from me.

"Wait, what? You built a cafe out of straw? How the hell do you do that?" She went on to tell me matter-of-factly how it's done and I listened, trying to imagine the bales of hay being roped with twine, stacked and made into walls.

After a few more minutes, I said it again. "Wait, what? You built an underground bed and breakfast? How the hell did you do that?" She described in vivid detail how she and her husband used a shovel to move thousands of pounds of dirt over the course of fifteen years before they finally brought in a small machine to do the rest of the work for them. Her matter of fact words had me spellbound as I sat in utter amazement of this woman who moved mountains to create the life she lived.

As she continued, there I was a third time. "Wait, what? You and your family would go hunting every Friday night for kangaroo because you had no food and you were known for your kangaroo pie that you sold at your straw cafe for the guests in your underground bed and breakfast?!" You get the idea. I was in the presence of a Goddess, a Warrior Woman, a High Priestess, an Avatar who would go on to expose her heart to me in a way that I knew I would honor and hold sacred for my entire life.

Mark was the third person who was staying in the luxurious retreat space with its floor-to-ceiling windows and sun-soaked patio. We knew he was spending Thursday night in Beverly Hills and wondered who he was and what brought him here. When he joined us on Friday morning for the first day of the retreat, a slender and healthy looking sixty-something man, we learned that Mark was a funeral director and had just written a book, "Living & Dying: Finding Love & Hope in the Journey of Loss." When Mark first walked in the door he seemed a very cool and collected man; not much emotion showing through, but just enough to feel some warmth and an eagerness about the group that was forming.

I told him how fantastic it was that he had written a book and what an amazing opportunity he had to help people with such a tender subject. I am no stranger to grief. Ever since my two sisters each lost their husbands at a young age, along with my own losses, I've had a very acute sensitivity to grief, loss, and transition. This common ground quickened my connection to Mark as we settled in. Last to arrive was Kat, a massage therapist with her New Zealand accent and sun kissed California skin.

As the four of us awaited Kyle's arrival on that first day of the retreat, I found myself getting emotional. I still couldn't quite believe this was all happening and how fast it happened. Kyle's lead facilitator who had communicated with me in Alaska, Kara, was waiting with us and informed us that Kyle had just texted and was on his way. I was standing by a large window overlooking the driveway when I saw him pull in.

Kara went to the door to meet him and I heard the voice I had come to know through countless hours of video watching. As he climbed the steps to the living room area, I started crying. As he welcomed us one by one, he was clearly bewildered by my tears when he gave me a hug. A pretty funny sight in retrospect, but at the time what else could I do? We moved to one of the three living rooms and gathered around a glass coffee table. We took turns sharing why we were there. I finally got to tell him this incredible story. As I finished, he said something that I'll always remember.

"Wow, I'm really honored. Thank you. But you know this is you, right? You know this is inside you?" I was perplexed by his comment and confused as to why he was making this all about me. Slightly annoyed, I shrugged it off as we started our weekend together.

After introductions and dinner, Kyle took us through an exercise where we divided a piece of paper in half: on the left side we wrote down everything we want to do and then on the right side we were to write the reason we can't do it. Of course, writing all my heart's desires on the left side of the page was a joy.

That had been how I started this new year, identifying all the things I really wanted to experience so the list was fresh in my mind:

I want to go on vacation on a beach

I want to help my family

I want to help people awaken to their magnificence

I want to be fully in my gifts and feel successful at expressing them

I want to have a steady income doing what I love

I want to fall in love

On the opposite page I wrote the "buts" that got in the way of my heart's desires. I knew them all too well. I want to go on vacation but I don't have the money. I want to do ___ but I can't because ___.

Ugh. Given what I had just been through in New Jersey with that trip to Maui I didn't take, I'd been more sensitive to how my mind played the role of Debbie Downer to my heart. I already know this game, I thought. Yet, as I was writing the "buts" to all my desires, I could feel this instant discomfort that grew in intensity quite quickly, and suddenly I wanted to run out of the room. What was happening? It was a very heavy, oppressive feeling and my head started to hurt immensely. Kyle was going around the group to check in. As people were talking, I was consumed by this horrible feeling, my tears building, my head exploding, my heart breaking. Then a tsunami-sized wave of emotion began to rise up, much like nausea - you know what's coming and there's nothing you can do but hold on. At some point I blurted out, "I need help!" Kyle turned around and I had a complete and total meltdown; huge drops of tears fell down my cheeks onto my journal pages. At the peak of my embarrassment, Kyle asked me what was going on and my answer was filled with sheer terror as if someone was about to drown.

"I have to know what I'm doing, what I'm supposed to do next. I have to leave here with a plan because if I don't have a plan, I won't know what to do and if I don't know what to do, then I can't make any decisions and if I can't make any decisions, then I'm going to go broke and the whole thing will be for nothing and I'll be a complete failure!"

As the words spilled out of my mouth I heard the absurdity of it all. I couldn't even believe I had just said that. That wasn't going to happen. What the fuck was I talking about? But the pressure of "getting it right" and coming home with a tangible plan that would give me the answers I was looking for, that would set out my calendar for the next three months (if not year), that would answer the years' long question about whether or not I should do another radio show that paid, when I should go back to New Jersey, where, if at all, I should get a job, what to teach again, what event to do...was crushing me. The release I felt vomiting it out of my mouth was unmistakable.

My goddess, what was I doing to myself? So much pressure to get it right, to figure it out, to have clarity. Clarity. Gotta know. Gotta have answers. That's what I believed I needed, clarity, which meant I believed I didn't have it. In fact, I was confused, which was clearly a problem when you're supposed to have clarity. No wonder I cracked. Who could live under such pressure? And don't tell me that stupid thing about the pressure needed by a piece of coal to become a diamond. I didn't want a fucking diamond. I wanted a clear path to a successful life - and not just any life, my successful life.

I was mortified by this outburst. I just couldn't believe it was happening. It felt like I had an enemy inside me. As Kyle worked with me, I kept calling this voice, this entity, this thing "she" - not wanting to be her, pushing her away, resisting the mess. My judgement of what was happening was so harsh, I wanted nothing to do with it. Kyle kept asking me "How do you feel?" but it was all in my head and I was getting so angry at him for asking me that stupid question over and over again. How was it not obvious how I felt! I did my best to stay present as the strength of what was happening pulled me apart.

(As I was writing this book months later, I could feel my mind trying to reach back into that night to remember what else happened, but I couldn't. There was this mental expectation as I wrote that I had to capture everything and that simply wasn't possible. I mean, how could I have maintained the writer's focus with all that was going on inside of me? I was on some sort of trip, so deep inside the caverns of my body, my mind, my heart, my soul, my life, that whatever senses I used to retain and recall were nowhere to be found that night. Because of that meltdown, I learned so much about my mind, the way it thinks, and how sabotaging it had been all this time.)

I wanted Kyle to take it away. He looked at me the whole time, holding a tremendous presence, unwavering to the power of the voice that was coming through me, blaming him. He had no attachment to it at all.

"What's she saying?" He asked me to listen to my separated self, the child version of me that I said was having this experience. "Easy for you to say." I told him. He explained something about a mother and a child and how the mother doesn't let the child lead, as that's what the mother is supposed to do. I could barely hear him, the pounding in my head was so loud.

I started to calm down and I stopped crying so intensely. I started to breathe. I began to feel better, but nowhere near good. My heart was in pieces all over the million-dollar floor and it hurt. I was exhausted and sad, so very sad that I had put such unbelievable pressure on myself, pressure to get "it" right, to make the right decision, to create the right event, to go and come at the right time, to use the right marketing words, to send the right email that people would read; on and on and on it went.

Those beautiful people held such a profound space for me that first night. I mean, nobody knew what the hell was going on! Here we were, selected for this transformational weekend and sequestered in this gorgeous home in L.A. with this man that we trusted, though we really didn't know. Hours into it, we were like fresh Alaskan salmon just pulled from the cold water and thrown onto the cutting table, the point of a sharp knife slicing us open to give full exposure to our hearts, bellies, and guts. In the other room, hummus, apple slices and almond butter awaited our emotional eating after we were all done. The contrast was crazy. The phrase, "What the fuck?" was uttered, whispered and shouted many, many times that weekend as we cracked open who we were and began to expand and change.

Transformation is messy. Death is scary. Birth is painful. The truth was that the first significant event of the weekend happened for me in those early hours, though I never would have admitted it, let alone been conscious of it. It would take a bit of time to understand exactly what had happened there.

Chapter 4

The Dark Night of the Soul

After everyone left and the house grew quiet, Sacha and I went to the kitchen. She'd had her own breakdown that night as well and was feeling pretty wiped out herself.

"Man do I wish I had a glass of wine right now," I said. Seconds later we heard Mark coming down the steps with a brown bag in his hand. "Do you prefer red or white?" he asked us. "Oh, how wonderful it is to have a man who knows what a woman wants," I joked, and we laughed as we took our seats around the marble counter.

"I'll take red," I said. Beneath the joking, I was reeling from the events of the day and I had a massive headache. We sat around the hummus, grapes, and chia chips, snacking mindlessly. I tried to sip the lovely liquid, but the truth was, I wanted to take the edge off quickly. I had already felt enough for one day. For another hour, if not more, Sacha and I listened to Mark tell his story. We felt a kindred spirit with Mark, the only man in our group. Older and just as eager to shed the dead layers of skin from his life, he welcomed our insight and feedback as we listened deeply and with compassion to his reason for being there.

As he spoke we could feel his heaviness, how weighed down he was with his own belief in his unworthiness – something we could both relate to. He confessed his need to always try to please and seek approval and be the right husband, father, boss, son. I lined up the organic green grapes on the cool marble counter, each representing these titles and burdens he was carrying. "This one is the good enough father, this one the good enough husband, this one the good enough boss, the good enough son. What if there was just this one? The good enough Mark?" For emphasis I plopped a grape in my mouth. We all laughed and toasted to being enough. As we climbed the steps to our individual bedrooms, utterly exhausted, we were also supported by the power of kinship and love and compassion that turned strangers into friends in just hours. It had been a rough day for all of us - but at the end of the night, we had each other. Whatever journey we had just begun, we were going together and that was enough to feel willing to do another day.

Upstairs in my bedroom, cradled by the most wonderfully decadent comforter and pillows, I sank into the support and tried to make sense of what had happened and what was going on. I was completely wiped out and blown away by what transpired hours earlier. Nothing was looking the way I had thought it would. My mind could not reconcile what I came to get with what I was actually getting, and how unbearably different the two were. Little did I know, my mind's perception of how things should look was only beginning to do its death dance.

I laid in that foreign bed with my cracked open soul. Before Kyle had said good-bye to us hours earlier, he had been so compassionate and supportive and clear about how I needed to take care of myself and to be gentle with myself and to love myself. That much I knew. Whatever was happening, it was requiring a tremendous amount of self-love and I was grateful that I had already gotten a bit of a handle on that almost nine years earlier.

Self-love came as a byproduct of nearly calling it quits after five significant losses over the span of eight months, from the fall of 2008 to the spring of 2009. First I lost my father, followed by my lover of seven years, my business partner, my beloved dog/child, and then my job. I was as close to dead as a living person could be, completely disintegrated, nothing but dust. I walked around and put up a good enough front so that most people didn't notice the light had gone out inside of me. It was just a matter of time. The dark night of my soul sparked by those losses went on for eighteen months. The entire time, I slept on the couch upstairs in my own house, unable to sleep in the bedroom where I had spent all those nights with the man I loved while our Buddy laid curled up in a ball on the floor next to the bed.

I remember the night a concerned friend came over and took all of my sharp knives with her when she left. *That was probably a good thing*, I thought as she drove away. I did get very close to taking my own life that winter in the womb of darkness that only Alaska can bring. The cold of the Arctic turns the tree branches into crystals and makes the air unbelievably still, frozen in time, the Northern Lights dancing across the sky above offering the promise of something magical and alive, yet so far out of reach.

Another friend had given me a full bottle of codeine before all this started happening, just passing it on casually to put inside my earthquake preparedness bag in case we had a "Big One" and anyone needed that level of care. That winter, I did. The ground-crushing tremor of death and despair that had flattened the infrastructure of my life registered high on the Richter scale. In yet another night of numbness, I arrived at the scariest part of choosing to end my life, which was my brain presenting me with the facts that I couldn't argue with. I'm good, I thought. I've loved, I've had success, life has been great. I'm good with this. I simply can't live with this pain any longer. This isn't life. I poured the merlot into a tall water glass and scattered the pills on the table. Hopelessness is the last rung on life's ladder; stepping down, there's nothing more. Nothing is emptier than feeling hopeless.

As I stared at what lay before me, I glanced to my right and saw pictures of my family, my mom, my sisters, my nieces and nephews. In a split second, my heart previewed what a horrible thing this would be for them. I could feel my mind change itself. *You can't do this. You can't do this to them.* My Catholic guilt came out of nowhere and put up its dukes. I was so angry that I couldn't end my pain without causing theirs. I put the pills back in the orange plastic bottle, snapped on the white cap and drank the rest of the wine.

The grip of Alaska's long winter began to soften as the days passed and brought the sun back with them - minute by minute, day by day, my house filled with light. I decided then that if I was going to live, I would live my life. My real life, the life I wanted to live, came here to live, the creative life that I hoped was still inside me, the dream I hoped had not vanished with the darkness of winter. One seemingly random night, grace came upon me. I grabbed the pillow and blanket from the couch and went downstairs and opened the door to my quiet bedroom. I crawled into the cold bed. Spring was coming.

In the days that followed, I would learn how to take care of myself for the first time in my life. I would ask myself, "What do you need?" and would hear myself say "Water," and I'd go get myself a glass. "What do you need to do next?" "I need to take a shower," and I would go and do that. After my death and res- urrection, I had to start all over again. I didn't quite feel like the phoenix at that point, but I learned how to love myself in a way I had never done before. There was no one else that could. That feeling of power, of rising, would come much later, but the seeds of rebirth were in those beginning days of emerging from the chrysalis.

I learned that death can give many gifts, none of which I per- ceived as such at the time. Grief and sorrow were all-consuming, and simply making it through the day was all I could hope for. Eventually, I realized that one of the great gifts I received from my own death was learning how to make myself a priority, learning how to put myself first without feeling guilty about it, learning how to say no, learning how to not fill my time with meaningless stimuli so as not to feel, learning how to sit with myself and hold my tender heart while it broke open over and over and over again. I was laying a new foundation for my life because I had to - the fire of transformation had consumed everything. I felt like I was walking through smoldering ruins, finding corners of burnt pictures that gave me a window into what had been, but no longer was. I had to rebuild from just the materials that my heart and soul were giving me. It wasn't much, but at that point it was all I had.

As I came out of this vivid memory and returned to the moment and the breakdown I'd had hours earlier on this first night of the Flow Group weekend, I realized I at least knew how to hold myself and love this part of me that had come out with such force. There was no doubt about it. I was there to uncover whatever blocks were within me, holding me back. However, I had no idea that this was what had been awaiting me.

The chill of the memory made me tuck the comforter snuggly under my chin as my mind raced around the details of that first exercise: desires on the left page, and denials on the right. I was trying to make sense of it and kept coming back to the moment in which I called the resistance to my heart's desires "she." *That's "her" part in it all*, I thought: *I dream, "she" reasons, every single time.* Though I'd been able to "win" the mental wrestling matches every now and again, it was never without a fight, and the damage caused within myself was unmistakable and measurable. Little did I know, it would take all of that weekend and one hundred more days for me to really understand this. I lifted my laptop off the nightstand, pulled it into bed, and started writing, hoping I could process some of what I was feeling so that I could go to sleep. Here is what I wrote:

Ode to the Right Side of the Page

You got triggered today

in a big way

and you always do

when I let my heart lead

from the left side of the page.

You're the external personification of

all the doubt, concern, fear and worry.

You're the no, you can't, better not, it won't work.

Disbelief in the believer.

You had no other choice but to rear your beautiful head

when I began to feel

to dare my best self to come out and play.

You had no other choice but to bring all that you've got

to the right side of the page

cause that's what you do,

when I dream you scream

when I live you give me every reason why I can't,

you shame me, hold me back, pin me down

with one lie after another.

It was your job to come alive when I called forth my joy

when I unleashed my soul

when I launched my rockets of desire

you, like water, put out the fire.

You brought facts and numbers and reasons

I tried to argue but ran out of seasons,

You held court and made the case of why

I couldn't

shouldn't

can't

won't

for a time I let you win and gave you my power.

And nothing weakens me more than when you bring up money

or my many responsibilities

as if my dreams weren't my responsibility

or that they wouldn't bring me money

as if they're separate or outside of my good

convincing me that you're my good.

I can see now that I came to believe you

as you deceived me

pretending to care

I don't blame you though

don't fault or judge you

because now I can see

the real me

And just because you don't like it

can't see it, don't believe it, have reasons for it,

I can now say, "No more."

I'm ok with you being the way you are

because you're no longer the star

I know who I am.

I'm the left side of the page

where my heart says yes to the sage

the place where I'm most alive

where it feels most right

that's why you were holding on for dear life

But it's over

I see the truth.

I made you

all these years causing so many tears

cause all I've ever wanted to do

is live on the left side of the page

that's what puts me on the stage.

And all these other parts of me

that are exhausted by the game

confused by the shame

have come up to be loved

because in the end

as in the beginning

there is just the One.

And so the right became the left and the left became my heart and my heart became my yes and my yes became my everything.

Through my writing, something was beginning to make sense. I finally fell asleep.

Chapter 5
The Exorcism

I awoke early on Saturday morning with more to say.

And so though I didn't want you to be there yesterday,
you were.

Though I was embarrassed that it was happening again, it was.

Though I laughed at the ridiculousness of what you had to say

you still had a grip on me

ripped me

open

until I could see

there's not a she and a me

there's only me

there's only The One.

You gave of yourself yesterday

a sacrifice of sorts

coming up to come out

giving it one last shout

because you know

that I know

that love wins out.

So I love you

I do

"Then erase the line that has separated us," you plead

"And plant a new seed."

I see now this is mine to do.

I take back my power this very hour.

I'm picking you up and bringing you home

to live happily ever after on the left side of the page.

I closed my laptop and headed downstairs, excited to share with the others.

We started Saturday morning with yoga outside on the patio in the California sun. As soon as I laid my body down upon the mat, I realized how important this piece was. Much had been dislodged last night and I wanted to make sure it was moving out of my system. With each stretch and pose, I could feel an important integration of body, mind and spirit. I could feel myself come more fully into my body, and it felt good and right and necessary.

While I lay in Savasana, a profound awareness came over me...and there were those tears again. An overwhelming feeling of sadness came through me. I realized that this whole time I had never wanted to separate myself from my heart. I remembered the video I submitted to be considered for this retreat and how I said that all I wanted to do was to live from my heart all the time. What I had really been saying was that I wanted to come back to it, to the left side of the page. All of this was happening so I could get what I said I wanted. I orchestrated my own breakdown so as to have this breakthrough. Uniting my body, mind and spirit through yoga was the final catalyst for this multi-process healing. Like it always does for me, yoga brought it home.

After yoga, Kara played a message for us that Kyle had recorded earlier. Another sweet, supportive, loving message with a specific call out to me to continue to be gentle with myself, and a mention of "her." I was looking forward to telling him about the healing that had just happened.

We went into an hour-long meditation and after thirty minutes or so, I was no longer a body, no longer in time, but mostly in space. I went somewhere, and it was the Universe. I merged with that infinite love and eternal potentiality. I was suspended in my masquerade. At one point, I heard this intense sound. It was my own breath. It was such a distinct timbre, at once the sound of my first breath and last. It was that breath that brought me back into my body, back into time and space, back into the density of matter, though I was still feeling out of this world.

Soon afterwards, I could hear the front door open and Kyle's voice brought us back to opening our eyes. Everyone had gone deep in their meditation experience, and we all needed some time to ground back down to earth. Water and food, a shower for someone else, I had to pee. When we came back together, we were still finding our way when Kyle asked us his most famous question: "How are you feeling?"

I told the group about the writing and what I came to understand because of it and what had just happened on the yoga mat. That realization was still buzzing inside me and the beauty of it was still settling into my cells. I felt so proud of myself, both that I asked for help last night and held on for dear life while I got it. Feeling better, I had come through a very big piece of why I wanted to come to this event in the first place and was ready to get on with today's focus which was mapping out the "Why" of my business. I was ready to move on, dig deep into the reason my business existed, and what I hoped to offer the world through it.

But my inside work wasn't over. I was calling in my own exorcism. Much to my dismay, my anxiousness returned as we moved through the second day of the retreat. My mind was working overtime, whispering in one ear all the reasons why I came here while shouting in the other all the things I was not getting. This led to a discussion around confusion, a topic where I was feeling very much like an expert. At one point, Kyle was explaining to me how my need for clarity was preventing me from loving my confusion, which he said would actually help me have clarity. I had no idea what the fuck he was talking about.

Needless to say, my head was exploding again. I tried to follow him, but everything was upside down and it hurt. At the same time, a sliver of understanding was taking shape within the rubble of my thoughts and expectations. I couldn't really focus on it because the more he talked, the worse I felt as I realized this truth: I am confused. More tears flowed. How was this possible? How was it that the desire for clarity, the very thing I came here to get, experience, understand, and know, was actually blocking me from achieving clarity? I was in tremendous resistance to it all and I was getting angry. To make matters worse, everyone else understood exactly what Kyle was saying! They were clearly seeing what he was trying to get me to see. I squirmed in the oversized leather chair and, once again, wanted out.

Kyle moved to the edge of the couch he was sitting on and looked me in the eyes, wanting for me to understand what he saw. But in order to do so, to accept my own confusion, everything would have to collapse. I had worked way too hard to keep it all together; no way did I want to go through that. But the truth was, things were already collapsing. All the limiting constructs of my thinking, of how things "had" to be, of how I "had" to be, were falling atop themselves in that moment, like a building being demolished to make room for something new. My mind was doing everything it could think of to avoid implosion.

I don't remember what made Kyle get up during our exchange and grab his phone, but he did so to document my process as I tried to come to grips with all that was going on. At the time, I was appalled by the idea that he wanted to record me as I was losing my shit. Later, I wished the camera had been rolling the whole time, so I could see what happened. It was difficult to remember that transformational moment because - very much like giving birth - it took all of who I was to be present for what was going on. The part of the brain that remembers things so it can comb through them later is not an active component when the contractions begin.

But at that point and time, on the second day of our Flow Group retreat, I didn't like that Kyle was recording me. I worried about how my hair looked, what I was wearing. Did I look fat? I could hear my mother's voice in my head, saying, "You don't have any mascara on!"

"What are you doing?" I demanded as Kyle started to walk towards me. "I do radio. I don't do video." He laughed, continuing to capture my resistance, loving what he was getting. "How do you feel?" he asked, his grin widening. "I feel like you're not listening to me!" I said. The group erupted into laughter, Kyle included. He put his phone down and played back the recording. Then I was laughing as I watched myself put my hand up to his phone's camera, and tell him, with all the attitude this Jersey girl could muster, "I don't do video." Who knew I'd say that again and again as I looked into the camera of my own phone for 100 days?

That Saturday night, Kyle took us all out for a healthy and delicious dinner and we all had a great time. It was a huge relief to get out of the house and be with each other in a relaxed and social way. But when we returned after dinner and Sacha, Mark and I gathered around the marble kitchen counter once again, I found myself wondering when this was all going to get better. I confessed my concern. I had been thinking all day about something Kyle said in that first Flow Group video I watched back in February. I remembered him saying that during these weekend retreats, he helps people identify the Why and the How of their business. The Why and the How of a person's business has become a huge focus for today's entrepreneurs. The Why gets at the heart of what you do and is the starting point for the action plan, which is the How.

I asked Mark and Sacha, "Hey, did you guys get your Why today? Kyle said we were going to get our Why, the reason for our vision, our dream, our business, but I don't think I did. Tomorrow we're supposed to get our How. I don't know if I got my Why today, but I'm getting my How tomorrow because I gotta leave here with something!" Still clinging to my expectations, I was fierce in my determination to get what I came to get from this weekend.

Sacha tried to calm me down and soothe my fears, but I don't think it helped much. I had told my family and my friends in Alaska that I was coming home with answers, a plan, and a focus. I was going to have to give an accounting of this weekend that I had been so excited to attend. What was I going to say? What the fuck was I going to tell them?

Chapter 6
Fuck Clarity

On Sunday morning, we began with Kundalini yoga. It turned out that Kara was not only a fabulously talented woman, but also a yoga instructor. Dressed in her white attire, she led us through a lovely hour. While we were doing alternating nostril breathing, without warning, these big fat tears plopped out of my eyes. What the hell? Was I some sort of tear manufacturer? Where were all these tears coming from and when would they end?

Afterwards, we sat for another long meditation, a task that was mentally difficult in the way only an 80-minute meditation could be for an active mind. Kyle was running late, and I was distressed. Time was ticking away. Is this meditation? I thought, because this is fucking painful. My mind was so jacked up I wanted to unzip myself and bolt. We'd been sitting for a long time and I started fidgeting; others were moving as well. My mind was in full judgment mode about Kyle, where he was and why he was so late. At the height of my mind's tirade, the door opened and so did my eyes - and there was Kyle with a bouquet of flowers for each of us. Terrific. I felt a flash of shame for thinking about him the way I did.

We settled in and Kyle said that today we were going to talk about our How. Finally. "Every How has to come from your Why," Kyle was saying. Uh oh. I could feel the anxiousness that always comes up when I "have to get something right" and, make no mistake about it, I definitely had to get this weekend right. Coming from an upbringing where people got good jobs, my experiment as an entrepreneur was causing me some significant financial woes and those who loved me were concerned, and understandably so. I was concerned too. The solution? I needed to go home with a Why, a How, a plan...which means I had to go home with clarity. Clarity - clarity so that my life would make sense and I'd know what I was doing and this whole crazy thing would work – and yes, so I could show the people around me that I could be successful without a traditional full-time job.

Pressure was mounting.

When it was my turn for Kyle's focus, I was ready. I told Kyle about the women's retreat Shirley and I were collaborating on. He then asked, "Ok, tell me why I should send Kara to it?" I responded, but quickly began to fumble. He continued, "You're telling me your How, your marketing plan. I want you to tell me the Why: why should I invest in sending Kara, what is she going to get from this weekend?"

I was getting wound up. Many of my future plans were riding on having these retreats generate income, and now I was experiencing myself unable to answer basic questions about them. We talked more about the name of my business, This Awakening Spirit and the tagline, "Set your real self free." I loved them both and felt really good about the message. As Kyle talked about the audience I wanted to speak to and how using words like "trapped" might better resonate with them, my heart sunk. In that moment, my mind convinced me that I'd done it all wrong, that after spending these last three years giving it everything I had, that I still wasn't doing entrepreneurship "right", whatever that looked like. All I wanted was to have the same success I saw others having, but I couldn't feel further away from it in that moment.

I knew the importance of the Why. I had to do this work that kept calling me back and inspired me to help others. I got that and wanted to have this piece understood; however, it wasn't something that was coming from me easily. There were all these other things I knew how to do and could do well: be a radio personality, interview people, do audio production, teach, speak, facilitate workshops, create successful events, work a room like nobody's business...I mean, it was a pretty long list, and yet somehow my entire new business focus rested in the hands of being able to explain why Kara should come to my retreat. I just couldn't do it anymore.

While Kyle was trying to help me with my How, I had tuned him out. I wouldn't accept that the successful expression of my gifts and talents hinged entirely on me getting my Why right. In that moment, I was letting myself off the hook and it felt good. Like Kyle said the day before, "Let go of what's heavy." Well, needing to know the answer to his question in that moment was one of the heaviest things I was carrying, and I decided to put it down.

It was wild. Kyle was finally giving me what I asked him to give me and it was pissing me off. My brain was a ball of confusion - I couldn't gather it up if I tried. He saw me struggling. "Look. You want me to tell you what to do but I can't. I can tell you what I did but I can't tell you what to do. You have those answers. You've got all these expectations about how it's supposed to look and you're not loving what is. Try saying this: "I'm confused, and I love it." There was a long silence. I had been resisting his diagnosis since Saturday and, though I continued to present my case for needing answers, he continued to focus on my confusion. All I could think was, I didn't have as much confusion before I got here as I do now! And I paid for this?!

My mind made a last-ditch effort to avoid being hauled out of its safe place of blaming Kyle for my problem instead of accepting what he was saying. This was an epic battle of logic and feeling, of self-righteousness and self-love. Everyone in the room felt it, too. Kyle stayed sitting in an unbelievable state of compassion and empathy for what was happening within me and because of that, I could no longer resist the truth of what he'd been saying. Eventually, I could feel my resistance and exasperation crash into each other. As Springsteen sings, "refusal and then surrender".

"Fuck clarity," I said to the group. "What is clarity anyway? I'm confused, and I love it." Applause and laughter filled the room. I felt an instantaneous relief. My entire body released an enormous weight. Suddenly, grace.

Speaking in a soft, loving voice, Kyle gave me my prescription. "Congratulations. Accepting your confusion transmutes it, dissolves the resistance to what is." He mentioned Katie Byron's work in her fabulous book, "Loving What Is." Having used her approach in my own self growth, I understood what he was saying - how accepting my mental mayhem (instead of pushing against it) was indeed keeping me connected to myself. "Here's what I want you to do as a way to heal your confusion," Kyle said. "I want you to meditate for an hour a day, every day, for 100 days. And after that, I want you to roll a video about the experience and post it on Facebook." What?! An hour?!! That's my reward for finally surrendering? I'd been meditating for about ten years, on and off (most recently on), but never for an hour. I usually max out at about twenty minutes. An hour? How could I do an hour?

Then he asked his assistant, "Kara, are there any books on confusion yet? Check The Confusion Method." She grabbed her phone and did a quick search. "Nope." Next he told me, "I want you to start writing about this. Write about your confusion. There's a book here. No one has written a book yet on confusion as a way to clarity!" His excitement was starting to rub off on me, though it felt overwhelming. Resistance tried to counter but died in a whimper. Then he said, "Either you write a book about confusion, or I will." How well he knew me in such a short amount of time. Nothing like a challenge. I agreed to his terms, telling everyone, "No, I'll do it. Not that I'm competitive or anything." More laughter as I sealed my fate.

As the day grew into night, the others in the room received Kyle's time and attention as well. Watching Kyle give so selflessly of himself, I remembered that his fiancée was waiting at home, pregnant with their first child, that he had a book about to launch, and who knows what else on his plate - and yet, he was still there with us. The clock rolled past nine, and then ten o'clock, five hours past the official end to this weekend. It dawned on me – Kyle didn't need us, yet here he was, still with us. He wasn't leaving until each of us has this final time with him.

I was deeply moved by how much he cared. He said he was investing in us because he wanted co-leaders to join him in this evolutionary, revolutionary change. While we wrapped up, I looked at him and said, "You know what? It's almost eleven o'clock and you're still here, even though you don't have to be. You could have left hours ago but you're so committed to seeing us through this process that you're still here, even though you're fiancé is texting you, wondering what the hell is going on! The only way I can say thank you is to do what I said I'll do. Clearly, you see something I don't see and so I'll do it until I see it too." I gave him my word: "I'm in."

To close the deal, Kara recorded us all saying what we agreed to. For me, it was 100 days of meditating for an hour a day, making a video after each meditation and uploading it to social media and writing about my confusion. Truly the most absurd commitment I'd ever made, but at least I could say I got something from this weekend, although worlds away from what I thought it would be.

Chapter 7

And So It Begins

I woke up on Monday morning, my last day in L.A., completely fried. I struggled to sit up in bed for my first meditation and I set my phone's timer for one hour. I closed my eyes. Suddenly the enormity of my commitment began to sink in. One hundred days of meditating for one hour only to make a video afterwards of whatever I just experienced and post it on Facebook?! Holy shit, what had I said yes to? I'm sure at some point, I fell asleep because I woke up. But no matter - I did it. The timer chimed and, true to my word, I rolled video and posted it on Facebook.

Saying goodbye was not easy for Sacha and me. We had already said goodbye to Mark and Kat the night before at the end of our marathon twelve-hour final day of the retreat. It was surreal as we took pictures with Kyle and hugged. This morning I just felt raw. To go from this emotional cocoon back home to Anchorage was not something I was ready for. Though parts of the weekend had been painful, there was much that was not. To have gone so deep, so fast and to hold such a space for these tremendous and beautiful people who were willing to do the inner work to live their magnificence was unlike anything I'd ever done. I didn't want it to stop, and this ending felt abrupt.

Sacha and I were standing outside in the warm California sun waiting for my Uber driver to take me to the airport. "Sacha, what am I going to write about? I have no idea what I'm doing." In all her magnificence, she replied, "And that's exactly what Kyle wants you to write about. Just meditate, move from your heart and keep writing."

There was silence between us, the kind of silence that holds the ache of an unwanted good-bye. We were both kind of numb, though Sacha was feeling better than I. Her breakthrough on Sunday was miraculous and life changing. She'd released a lot of pain and was feeling lighter. We hugged and promised to see each other soon and talk sooner. As I drove away, I felt unbearably vulnerable and wished like hell she was coming with me.

Inside the packed LAX Airport, waiting, my mind was still going crazy...only now it was telling me, *Hurry up! Write it all down before you forget*! Oh great. Not only did I have the pressure of not knowing what the hell I was doing and feeling confused about my life, I also had the additional pressure of trying to write down everything that happened this weekend before I forgot.

Thirty-five thousand feet above the earth, and all I could tell myself was to keep writing. Kyle had said, "Give me 60,000 words," and I was going to do it. The mind chatter, though, was off the hook. I was doing something I'd never done before and my mind didn't like it. It had no reference point, no past to cling to. *Do you even know what the hell you're writing about?* Well not really, except that I did. I was writing about being confused, which was quite easy for me to do just then because I had never been more confused in my life.

It was so interesting how non-stop my thinking was. It was really extraordinary to be so aware of it, to observe how often my thoughts made me feel worthless or completely stressed out. I closed my laptop because I felt like I was pushing to write and thought, *No, let's just meditate a bit,* but moments later there it was, cracking the whip again and telling me to keep writing.

What if you forget? Then you won't have a book. Then you won't have the money. Then you won't have a life! Good grief, where did this stuff come from?

I remembered Kyle saying to me on Sunday that while I believed clarity was the answer to everything, what it created instead was mental stress - especially since I didn't have any clarity. Confusion resulted from going outside of myself to find whatever it was that I believed I didn't have. What was additionally interesting to me was that I knew this; my spiritual education taught me this. In fact, I was teaching other people this! And yet, here I was doing it.

In the few notes taken during the weekend, I wrote that my thoughts - specifically my questions - distracted me from my focus because they set me up to believe that I didn't know the answer, or I didn't know how to do something. They caused me stress because they made me feel I wasn't on the right path or I didn't know the right thing to do - or that I needed to figure something out in order for my business and my life to be a success. My questions caused delay. They caused me to second guess myself. Ultimately, they caused decision paralysis.

As the plane took me closer to home, I huddled in the middle seat with my sunglasses on, but they couldn't hide the tears. I was remembering how, over the weekend, Kyle had us do another exercise where we listed things we saw as positive and negative about ourselves. I had put my crying on the "Negative" list. Well, today I was redefining it as a "Positive". My crying was an asset. It was helping me release! My Goddess, the number of things we stirred up in three days was insane. We had completed such big work and I kept thinking how much better it would be if we were all still there having one more day. But I wasn't there. It was over, and I was heading home. In that moment I didn't even care if any of these thoughts of mine became a book. The sheer act of writing was therapy and that's what I needed most.

I touched down in Anchorage at 1:00 am, the frigid temperature of the night blasting through my California outfit as I waited for a taxi. Once back at the house, I took a hot shower and crawled into bed, desperately hoping for sleep as the night moved on. I was feeling shell-shocked. I'd been so happy before I left Alaska and now just five days later I was utterly depressed. What the fuck? There was a loud army of thought-soldiers marching across the field of my heart with unrelenting commentary:

So how is now any different than last week? At least last week you were excited; now you're crying. You thought you were coming home with all these answers and all this clarity and you still have no sense of what to do next. We still don't know when we should go back to New Jersey, what to do about an income, where to spend these last weeks or days or however long you're staying in Alaska before you move on again. You have no events, nothing to teach, no job, and instead you're writing what's supposedly going to become a book about the confusion method, and how loving your confusion leads to clarity!

In spite of the war of words raging in my head, I reached for my phone and set the meditation alarm for 7:00 am and Day Two of The Confusion Experiment.

The Video Transcripts

A Reader's Guide

Before I put this book together, I sat and watched my 100 videos back to back over the course of three days and realized something unmistakable. The Confusion Experiment was the equivalent of putting the camera in the chrysalis, and the transformation I witnessed was my own. Viewing this was a life-changing experience that brought forth an important question: how willing was I to let go of aspects of who I was so a greater expression could emerge? How willing are any of us? Too often we cling until stagnation sets in and the chance for birth dies in the womb of possibility. Willingness is key. In each of my videos, I witnessed myself as someone who was willing: willing to explore, willing to question, willing to let go, willing to show herself in the most vulnerable ways simply because of the possibility of insight, growth and healing through the revealing of Truth. Though there were countless times when I wanted to quit, and my mind made up some excellent reasons why I could go back on my word, I knew I had to keep going. I'm old school and my word means something. I couldn't quit and I'm grateful now I never did.

Fascinated by the transformation my videos revealed, I revisited one of the most studied transformations of them all: the caterpillar becoming the butterfly. The caterpillar dying to itself so the butterfly can live is such a sacred process. In reading an article about butterflies written by Daven Hiskey, I learned that in order for a caterpillar to change into a butterfly, the caterpillar releases enzymes that literally digest nearly all of its own body. After the digestion process, what's left inside the chrysalis is a very nutrient-rich soup from which the butterfly will begin to form. Within the goo that was the caterpillar are very tiny imaginal discs, which are similar to embryonic cells. These discs are actually present within the caterpillar its whole life, but they stop growing at a certain point and only start again when it is time for the caterpillar to morph into a butterfly.

This was so powerful to me. What this meant was that, within us, is a pre-existing template of perfection and wholeness and divinity that lies dormant, waiting. This is why growing with change and even initiating change is so fundamental to personal evolution. Once the proper time arrives, the imaginal discs of the butterfly-to-be use the nutrients from the digested body of the caterpillar to form different parts of the butterfly's body, with different discs becoming different tissues. Once the process is completed, nearly every part of the dissolved caterpillar's body is replaced with new parts, forming the butterfly. The imaginal cells put themselves back together into a new shape. This is exactly what happened to me. Meditation digested my mental body. My divinity emerged and reshaped me into who I've always been.

In my own experiment, this nutrient-rich soup was the stuff of the Divine that I was able to feel into more frequently because of meditation. This Divine nature is within us all. When we begin to stir this soup with self-help books, spiritual education and practices like meditation, the nutrients of our own divinity that have been waiting for us, begin to come into form as our real self. This is the self I'm seeking to help people set free.

Speaking of the Divine, I talk about Affirmative Prayer in the 100 Days. Day 48 touches on it, but I want to make sure you know what I'm talking about because it's a fundamental part of my life. It's powerful and it works. We live in a mental universe where thoughts have creative juice within them and become the stuff of our experience by the universal laws that govern all life (the Law of Attraction, the Law of Reciprocity, the Law of Mental Equivalents, to name a few.) The spiritual philosophy I embrace, The Science of Mind and Spirit which is celebrating its 100th year, teaches that a realization of humanity's unity with the spiritual nature of life sets this creative process in motion through our thinking. Thoughts transmit magnetic energy that attracts other energy of the same frequency. Affirmative Prayer is a direct, focused, and organized method that allows us to activate the Creative Process by consciously rearranging our thinking. It moves us from what we're experiencing and focusing on to how we want to feel about the situation. For example, I used to say, "Please God, help me find a job." Now I say, "I am guided to my perfect employment. I give thanks for my new job!" It's a simplified example but enough to help you follow what I'm talking about. Affirmative Prayer is speaking life into what you desire.

One more note about transformation: if one was to cut open the cocoon during this process, it would look like a complete mess. But do you know what's inside that mess? That which is seeking to emerge. So, if you feel like you're in chaos and the outrageousness of transformation is happening to you as well, try to remember that the seeds of change lie within your confusion. Divine timing is at hand.

~~~

You're about to read transcripts of the videos I made during my 100 days of meditation. The process began with my alarm going off and me sitting up in bed and meditating; however, it became obvious to me pretty quickly that I needed to actually get out of bed and sit in a chair or on a couch. Splashing water on my face was an added bonus. After I meditated, I picked up my phone, turned the camera toward me and just started talking. I never knew what was going to come through me, and many times I would say exactly that: "I don't even know what

I'm doing. I don't know what I'm about to say." But sure enough, things came up and out.

To make the reading experience more fluid, nuances of tone and gestures from the videos have been incorporated into the text. I have also taken the advice of my editing team to streamline the transcripts, something I initially resisted because I wanted you to have the raw experience of the videos that represented real time. However, I realized that, whereas the viewer was getting a video a day and had time to digest my daily transformation, you, as a reader, are moving through several days at a time, one right after another. This makes it necessary to tighten things up a bit without sacrificing the essence of what was happening. Lastly, the title used for each day's video is included. As a music lover and radio broadcaster, more times than not, a song title captured the essence of what I was talking about that day. And with that, I welcome you to The Confusion Experiment, an invitation that is both scary and exhilarating in its vulnerability. I'm really glad you're here.

The 100 Days

Day 1: I Have No Idea What I'm Doing

This is Day 1 of my 100 Days of Meditation, where I'm committing to an hour of meditation every morning, between 7:00 and 8:00 am, and making a video right after that. All of this is very much outside of my comfort zone – but that's OK, because I want to be in a new one, and this is what's going to make it happen.

I'm in California still, and I'm so exhausted. I feel like I just came out of a womb! I don't know what the hell happened this weekend, but I'm keeping my word. I've been in a Flow group with Sacha, Mark, and Kat, the most excellent Kyle Cease (and his phenomenal staff, Kara and Sarah). I really don't have words for it yet, but it was definitely challenging to stay awake in my meditation today. And that's OK! I did it.

Honestly, I feel as confused and chaotic right now as I was all weekend...and beyond that, most of my life. But I also feel some sort of incredible peace and calm, which I'm very, very grateful for. And so begins The Confusion Experiment.

Day 2: I Don't Know What's Going On

I have to tell you, I'm not really quite sure what I'm doing. I'm back in Anchorage, Alaska. I just feel really, really out of sorts today, and my mind is needing a lot of love. I'm blown away by the craziness and the incessant thoughts and perspectives and preferences, all this stuff that my mind is hurling at me. I miss the people that I spent the weekend with, and I have to really love myself today.

I'm not out of bed yet. I'm not up to par. I don't feel like I have a lot of energy. And of course, my mind doesn't feel like it came home with any answers or clarity, and all of this other ridiculousness. On this, Day 2 of my meditation challenge, I'm judging it against the meditations I did with the Flow group this weekend. I think that I have to make a slight adjustment to exactly what happens at 7:00 am. I might need to give myself permission to get up a few minutes earlier and just go sit in a chair versus sitting in the bed.

I don't know. Whatever. I don't even know why I'm talking to you like this, but Kyle told me to do it and I trust him. I trust that he has my best interest in his hands and he's wanting me to release my magnificence. But it kind of blew me away this morning that I just don't have any clarity. I can see now that I went to this weekend retreat really wanting clarity, wanting direction, wanting specific answers to specific questions. I was thinking about how we were talking about our businesses on Sunday, the projects, plans, and events we already have, and I was talking about my work with This Awakening Spirit, wanting to help people set their real selves free. Kyle said, "Well, what does that mean?" And I just hate that! I have such a strong reaction to that, when people start talking about marketing and being able to sell the Why. Why should someone come to these women's retreats? Why should anybody come to anything that I do?

Truly, I know that this stuff is important. But for several years, now, I've been trying to "figure out" the marketing language and "figure out" what to say and "figure out" the wording so it's the right wording, so that it touches the right people and it does the job, and people show up. It's frustrating that, after the time and work and money I've put into classes and learning about this, that I still didn't know how to answer Kyle's question.

And I'm just letting it go today. I'm being totally okay with that. I refuse to believe that the expression of my purpose is hinged on getting the right wording for some ad or website page. I have to let it go. The pressure is too immense.

Day 3: Dazed and Confused

It's Day 3 of The Confusion Experiment, and I'm still very confused. So it must be working! It is so uncomfortable for me to record myself looking au naturale: no shower, no makeup, no hair effort. Just me, as I am. This continues to be something that is really stretching me, and I don't like it at all. But I'm doing it anyway.

I feel very low-vibration again today. I don't feel happy. I don't feel joy. I was so off-the-hook excited when I found out I was selected to go to Kyle's retreat. Now I'm questioning, "Why were you so happy then? Why aren't you happy now?" The best thing I can do is acknowledge that I was overjoyed last week because something was happening that my heart had already predicted for me.

The other truth I'm sitting with is that I really thought I was going to go to this retreat and get some answers, action steps, or a roadmap. I thought I'd get clarity! Clarity about my life. Clarity about what the hell I'm doing. Clarity about the rest of the year. I had this overwhelming expectation around getting answers.

And I didn't. I didn't come back with answers. I don't feel like I have significant action steps. I do have this feeling of, what the hell happened? Is what happened enough for the time and money I spent? But it has to be, right? It has to be enough, because that's what happened. It's amazing to simply be in this awareness and to just love myself through it because chomping at my heels is a feeling of depression. It's a very familiar feeling that is so heavy and so sad, and I don't want to feel it. I tell myself, this isn't really who you are. This depression is coming up and coming out. It needs to be released.

I have to do some shifting today. I have to get some high-vibration language coming out of my mouth. I have to tell a story beyond the story that my mind is trying to tell me because it's not a good one. There's a pattern here. It seems that other people in my Flow Group are having a good time with what they learned, having good results already, and I'm not. As I speak, I'm becoming aware that there's a pattern of feeling left behind. The best thing I can do today is really love myself completely, keep writing, and stay on my creative edge.

Right now, I'm just wingin' it. I guess by definition that means I've got wings, so that's a good sign.

Day 4: Slip Sliding Away

I had a deep, intense meditation this morning. Though I've been meditating for many years, I can see that sticking to it for an hour is necessary if I want that depth. What I'm experiencing is about 35 minutes into the meditation, and it's something that I have not been able to touch when I meditate for 15 or 20 minutes a day. This is an interesting experiment, just for the meditation part alone.

I felt like I was having some sort of emotional shift in the meditation today, and I still feel it. I'm grateful for that. I've been thinking back about yesterday, and I think one thing that's for sure is that I'm eager to touch what's behind all these thoughts. I'm looking forward to piercing the veil, as they say, and being with the One that's behind me, the thinker.

Yesterday we got about 12 inches of snow here in Anchorage, and I was stuck in the snow for a very long time. Eventually these guys came by and kindly helped push me out. Before leaving they said, "Make sure you don't turn the wheel the wrong way," and sure enough, I turned the wrong way and got stuck again.

After 45 frustrating minutes I was finally free, and off I went into the streets. I'm driving a wonderful car that my friend gave me, a 1995 Buick. It has the kind of trunk you can fit four bodies in – it's so dang big! It has these luxurious, soft seats and I am glad to have it. Unfortunately, it's also about a half inch off the ground. Needless to say, I kept getting stuck and spinning out as I was moving about. I thought, *Isn't this symbolic? This is how I feel. Stuck, but also un-grounded.*

I made arrangements to borrow a friend's Subaru so I could get around safely. It took several hours to coordinate the drop off and slide my way out to where she was. When I saw her I cried from frustration and stress, and she was very comforting. She reminded me that she, too, has had conflict with her thoughts and that her thinking has put her in the hospital a few times. I didn't know that, and in an odd way, it was comforting to hear that somebody else was having that kind of relationship with their thinking.

I know I cry a lot, but man – something was going on with me. Yesterday I was also supposed to meet up with my great friend and collaborator, Shirley Mae. We had agreed on a time to meet and I was running late because of the snow and car swapping. When I got to her house hours late, I was a mess. She made me a cup of tea while I cried out my story about the weekend. "Kyle's telling me to write. Can you believe it? I'm having a breakdown and he thinks this whole thing is a book! The man is crazy!" Shirley sat on her red couch nodding her head and saying, "Uh-huh. Mm- hmmm." At some point, I start to hear her and realize, I'm not going to get any sympathy from her!

But she was really great. And because she was simultaneously able to hold some space for me while also speaking some truth to me, I began to shift. I began to realize, this is happening to me, but it's not who I am. Shirley got up, left the room and came back with a blank piece of white paper and some colored pencils. "Here," she said handing me the sheet. "Fold this in half." I resisted immediately. I knew exactly what she was trying to do. "No way, Shirley, I'm not doing it." She would have none of it. "Fold this in half," her tone was serious, and I obliged. "Now, take a pencil and write, The Confusion Experiment by

Camille Conte." Like a child stomping its feet, I begrudgingly followed her instructions. "Now, open it and on the inner page write, "Forward by Kyle Cease"." By this time, I was laughing at the ridiculousness of it all. I felt better by the time I left.

So today, I feel a little lighter. I'm going to start telling a different story; I think that's important to do. Ninety-six more days to go...I've got time.

Day 5: Just the Tip of the Iceberg

This morning I'm very sensitive to my thinking.

My meditation was very deep, again. I don't know what the hell was going on! I came out of it, but then I fell right back into it. It was quasi-meditation and quasi-sleep at that point, because I was still sitting upright. I hope that, like with any practice, it will become a little bit easier to do. And, I'm celebrating that I did it. I felt peace and calm in a lovely way.

Yesterday was a much better day, and last night was yet another great blessing because I have these incredible friends in Alaska. I had dinner with two of them, Terry and Mary Kay, who wanted to hear all about my weekend. It was magnificent, because they're very aware and active-in-their-consciousness kinds of people. They're always seeking to be and become their best selves and are tremendous supporters of what I do.

It was a very engaging conversation. The point is, I've talked to a few people about my experience and – lo and behold – I'm not alone. Others are engaging in this topic of confusion, mental chaos, the thoughts, and the thinker. This is all very exciting right now. I feel like an iceberg of thoughts and fears got dislodged and floated away. I can feel that much of the crying I was doing was because the iceberg was leaving. I cried because of everything I thought I needed, everything I thought I needed to understand, everything I thought I went to get from my weekend in California. The tears were the release of all that. They came first from a place of sadness and depression that

I didn't get those things, and then from a place of relief.

But today it all feels different. Now I have a sense of eagerness about this 100 Day experiment.

Day 6: Two for One

There's a definite point in this hour-long meditation where my head starts to tingle. I see these lava-like globs of purple color and it's seemingly happening when I reach the point where I'm not thinking as much as I was prior to that moment.

Today the thinker (my own mind) is very active. I sit there in my meditation and just observe and wait for that moment when my head starts to tingle, because that's when I start to slip into something else. And the next thing I know, I'm not thinking about when this is going to be over or why did I ever agree to this experiment. Those thoughts slip away, and the next thing I know, the timer is going off.

I spent some time with another very dear friend, Allen yesterday and now I'm acutely aware of the language of my thoughts. I was listening to him share things that were very similar to what I've been saying: that our thoughts present our lives to us and make us feel like we should be worried for some reason or other. We should worry because we don't know everything, because we don't have a specific plan, because we might not be living the 8-5, Monday-through-Friday lives, because we seemingly don't have the kind of security that others have. Pick your poison.

Today is April 1st, day of fools, and I'm just sitting with this and I'm allowing all of it. I'm very excited to get to some writing today. I feel the need to get to that and share more of this awareness, or whatever this thing is.

Yesterday I did my radio show and I brought up this idea I've had, about either changing the format of the show or maybe doing a second show. I woke up this morning and was like, *Oh my god! What are you doing, bringing your inside process to your listeners? Why did you do that?* There goes my mind, being fearful and criticizing the desires of my heart. I decided to speak directly to this voice. I know "she" is not separate. This was me I was talking to. I put my hand on my heart, as Matt Kahn teaches, saying out loud, "I love you. I love you."

One week ago, I was in L.A. with Kyle and the Flow group, not getting what I thought I needed to get. Instead, I was being cracked open in a way I didn't want to be. Since that time, I can sense that even more has been softened - even more has broken away, and more space is being created for something to emerge. I don't know what that is, but I can feel it. I trust that it is happening without my oversight and control. In the meantime, I'm continuing to speak love to myself and I'm asking myself, "What do you need? What do we need to do next?" I move forward from those responses.

It's April Fool's day. What does a fool believe? Well, I feel like I've been face to face with my fool for at least eight days now, and I love her.

Day 7: Breakup

Here in Alaska, we're inside a season we call Breakup. Breakup is when the temperature rises and things begin to melt. The enormous amount of snow that has fallen this year has begun to turn to piles of slush. These incredible, weapon-like icicles that have been hanging from buildings are now dangling, hanging on by a thread of ice, as everything is going back into its original form: water.

I'm relating to this. It's how things feel internally: messy and slushy. I have to slog my way through knowing that, eventually, something wonderful is going to be born from the muck and mess. I have a sense of that time which is coming, the time where the snow is gone, the grass begins to show itself, and the trees begin to bud. There's a feeling of life and energy and hope. That's what I'm knowing today, that - in the midst of this experiment that I definitely did not want to do today - I'm in

Breakup. It took many hours to get through the single hour of my meditation because things got messy and sloshy. I had to stomp my way through it all to get to this. But I did!

Today I'm going to use the wonderful ideas from the spiritual teacher Esther Hicks and tell a story that raises my vibration. I'm going to take a drive and let this amazing place do what it has always done: fill my soul with its majestic beauty.

I'm also appreciating a conversation I had with Kara, Kyle's assistant. I texted her earlier this morning because I felt like I was losing my shit, and she called me. She listened and shared some thoughts. She helped me see how I have valued my mind and confused my thinking with the Mind that knows all.

In truth, they couldn't be more different. My mind can lay out the argument and absolutely convince me that THIS (whatever this may be) is The One Right Thing, and seconds later it can lay out another argument and convince me that it isn't. So yeah...perhaps it's not the best guidance system to depend on.

Day 8: A Little Help from My Friends

I just finished my first video call with Sacha, who's back home in Australia. I mentioned to her that I didn't do my meditation video this morning because I moved from one house-sitting job to the next and my phone died, but I left my cord at the other house. Though I finally found another one and had charged my phone, I had decided to just make tomorrow Day 8. She so sweetly said, "Alright. Or you could do it right now." So, I'm doing the video for Day 8 even though it's night time.

This morning, I don't even think I had opened my eyes - I was just barely conscious – and bam! All these thoughts were right there. I couldn't believe how many of them were waiting for me. I thought, *Man, how does this work? Do these things just swim around in a pool all night long and then, as soon as somebody wakes up – ZOOMP – they go right into the person?* While meditating, I was more acutely aware of these thoughts. I'm starting to really feel how I am not those thoughts.

After talking to Sacha, I feel grateful. I feel lighter, the way I do anytime one butterfly talks to another butterfly and they get to flap their wings together for a bit. The four of us from the Flow Group are all going to talk on Wednesday and I'm excited to see everyone else and catch up. It's a wonderful thing to be traveling along with this committed group of people who are ready to say yes to their heart and their magnificence and to whatever is wanting to emerge. Sometimes that isn't easy to do. I loved myself through these last several days; they were really quite intense. And, today is a better day.

Day 9: The Womb of Creation

When I went into my mediation this morning, I asked to be taken into the womb. Today is my birthday, and I wanted to just travel into my mother's womb and remember what that was like. It was really a remarkable and beautiful experience. I was nestled in the womb of the Universe. I was seeing me as this tiny, curled up, cocooned baby who was fully sourced, being given everything she needed to live, and had this beautiful and amazing host. It was so peaceful just to be suspended in that liquid love of Life itself.

Then suddenly, the contractions were coming and it was wild to be inside the womb when it was time for me to be born! The discomfort, pressure, difficulty and the pain of going from where I was into where I was going was tremendous. The next thing I knew, I was outside, looking at my head crowning, then watching my shoulders come out. It was pretty intense. This baby was placed on her mother's stomach and just held and loved. I feel a deep connection to that journey today. I love my mom and my dad. I know we chose each other.

I still don't like the vulnerability I feel doing these videos after such a beautiful meditation.

Day 10: The Morning After

Things did not go according to plan. I was out late last night enjoying my birthday, and as a result I did not hear my alarm or the early phone call from Kaleem, my Wednesday-morning prayer partner. I didn't get into my meditation until about 8:30, and then the phone started ringing with stuff I needed to deal with, and I had to take those calls. I've only really gotten about a half hour in today, but I wanted to get my video done and be accountable to what I'm doing.

I am slightly horrified by the idea that I have to do 90 more of these videos. I can't say that I like it anymore today than I did on Day 1. My mind remains active about what it thinks I should be doing and saying, and it's all just so interesting. Today I'm realizing that my life is calling me to do some things differently. One of them is to try to get to bed earlier at night. I tend to be a very late-night person but I can see that how I start my day changes dramatically, even if I'm able to get to bed by 11 or 12. This is better for me, and much earlier than I normally go to sleep. The other thing is that I'm going to release some online courses I created a few years ago and make them available at no cost. I think it's time to set them free and see if they help people.

Day 11: The Deconstruction of the Mind

In my meditation this morning, I realized that clarity and needing to have answers and direction – they're all constructs of the mind to make the ego feel like it's in control. In reality, it's just made up. We're so obsessed with needing to know and having a five-year plan and goals and vision boards. There's an idea that we need to be able to answer all the questions about what we're doing with our lives. It's so stressful. But for me it's also boring; this automated way of living hasn't inspired me for a really long time. Maybe I'm dealing with the final pieces that have to fall away. I have lived from my heart-space, and I know the heart is where The One resides. I know that's where the Big

Mind lives. When I went to the weekend retreat with Kyle, I said, "I want to live from my heart all the time." But in order to do that, I can see how these constructs of my mind have to be loved and released.

That's what's been happening – the deconstruction of this whole way of being and living. I've been in my heart space and doing all these things for the last three years: traveling, teaching, caring for my mom, and trying to launch into the world with my gifts and talents reorganized in a way that allows something new to emerge. This morning I'm realizing that "knowing" is just a distraction. For me, right now, it's about coming home to my heart and allowing it to inform and inspire me. "Live from your heart" - what does that mean? What has to fall away? Where can't you live anymore if you want to live from your heart? How does this change things? How does it change me? What's trying to emerge from the place that keeps calling me back to it?

I'm once again seeking to establish something that's different for me. All I can do is keep trying and set myself up to do the best I can. I don't always do it. It's important to love that and just try again without any blame, shame, criticism, or beating myself up. None of that. It's time to really love ourselves and be gentle with ourselves and stop needing to improve something that's already perfect.

Day 12: Holding a Space of Love

I just can't help but continue to marvel at the symbolism of the Breakup going on outside with Mother Nature, and the Breakup that's going on within me. It's actually immensely supportive to witness that which is happening inside myself mirrored in the outside world. It makes me feel like I'm right where I'm supposed to be. There is a time, a season, and a reason.

All day long, the sun shines on these massive blocks of snow hanging from the roof and there's a non-stop dripping of water. There's an actual visual of something solid turning into something liquid from the heat of the sun. Maybe these hour-long meditations are similar to the heat of the sun for me. At certain times of the day, there's been enough melting and loosening for huge slabs of snow to rumble off the roof and hit the ground, and right behind it is another slab. That's how it's been feeling for me. There are huge chunks melting and falling away and space is opening.

Last night was a remarkable evening. I was in the presence of three other very high-consciousness people. There was a lot of energy moving in the room. I realized that our hearts are cracking open for all sorts of reasons. It's happening no matter who you are – whether it's private or public, expressed through tears or anger. Our hearts are breaking open.

One of the most important things we can do is to simply stay with ourselves as the emotions rise up from all the places where we've stored them to deal with later. This isn't always easy or pleasant. However, we get the opportunity to witness this process and hold our tender hearts. We get to witness the iceberg breaking and floating away. We can also hold this space for each other. Don't judge the moment if it happens for you or somebody else. Just absolutely love on each other.

Speaking of loving ourselves, creating these videos has helped me decide that I'm done with making disparaging comments about my looks. That's been a very long-held oppression against myself, and I'm not doing it anymore. I'm ready to reclaim all the truth about myself and my beauty. I'm not going to let those voices and those thoughts communicate anything less than I am enough, and I love myself exactly as I am.

Day 13: The Now of the Heart

My meditation didn't happen until 9:00 pm today. And, I still did it. Things are shifting. I'm noticing that I am receiving insight and – dare I say – clarity.

Afterwards, I went for a walk and was asking myself, what are we going to do? I'm not feeling it here in Anchorage right now. The plans I've made have been falling apart. Projects are stalling. What is going on, what am I doing, and where am I going? In my mind I was writing the pros and cons list. Then I realized...oh my gosh! I'm trying to make a decision and plan from the past, from what I've already done. I realized that is not necessarily what I want to do. I have been doing that and it's not working right now.

Suddenly, I thought about this book and the writing that I've been working on. I thought, *What if I just locked onto this writing and really gave these next 45 days everything I could give it? What if I went back to New Jersey and helped my mom for a six-week phase and got some basic chop wood/carry water jobs?* I tell you what, my entire body lit up and got electrified. I felt immediate lightness and excitement and thought, *This is our inner guidance system giving us a big YES.* It was powerful, and guess what? I feel like I have some direction.

I know these hour-long meditations are doing something wonderful. I know that things shift when we keep showing up for what is and accepting what is. I know how important it is to keep holding our hearts and surround ourselves with good people who listen when we're losing it. I know that Mother Nature shows us how, with enough sunlight, that which is ice cold and hardened eventually begins to melt and break away, making room for something else to emerge.

Day 14: The Grab

It's already late in the evening, though it's still light outside. This is how Alaskans measure the return to spring. If the sun is still up after 5:00 pm, it's a good sign. The days are getting longer here in the Great Land.

However, today wasn't a great morning. I'm releasing old trauma from my body. This release started back when Trump's pussy-grabbing conversation with Billy Bush came out. I mean seriously? His name is Billy Bush? After that happened, I was on

Twitter and stumbled upon writer Kelly Oxford sharing the first time she was sexually assaulted, and others followed suit. I began reading, and I was pulled into the momentum of this universal experience as women all over the world told their stories of assault in 144 characters.

My own story rose swiftly from its perch in the depths of my unconscious. I left my body as the entire scene played out in my mind. In 1983, I was thrown to the ground while waiting for the New Jersey PATH train. I was standing alone on an outdoor platform and this man came up from behind me. He knocked me down to the cement, punched and slapped me, and was on top of me, grabbing my pussy. As he began to unzip my pants, a whistle blew in the distance and he jumped off and ran. The train pulled up and, as the doors opened, I stumbled inside. I was traumatized by the memory and it really shook me to my core. This is why I marched in the Women's March In Washington D.C. That's why Inauguration Day was very difficult for me. So now I'm just loving myself and holding this space for myself, and hoping that – in allowing it to come up – it's being released, forever.

Day 15: Listen Deeply

My impulse today is to remain quiet and to listen deeply and to stay connected with nature. I'm staying out of the headlines, the news, and off social media – aside from posting my after-meditation video. I want to continue to keep my vibration high by being mindful of all that I am so grateful for and for the many blessings that fill my life, to see of how I can be of service to people and to my community today.

These are tender days. I'm going to follow the counsel that I've received this morning in my meditation, which is to simply listen deeply.

Day 16: Full Moon Fever

It's 8:00 at night on a full moon eve here in Anchorage, Alaska – the land of the midnight sun. I'm looking at this moon – almost as bright as daylight – thinking of that Springsteen song: "Mama always told me not to look into the eyes of the sun, but Mama – that's where the fun is."

I clearly need to refresh my commitment to this meditation project because I have a story, and the story is that I'm not a morning person. Waking up and sitting up in bed is not necessarily working. I did that this morning and everything was good until, the next thing I knew, I woke up. That's not what I want to experience.

I have to actually get out of bed, have a glass of water, and sit down somewhere else. I want to do this right. By "right" I mean that I want to do this in a way that will bring to me the fullest experience possible. Things are happening and I have seen and felt a difference since I've been meditating for an hour every day. I guess one of the things I've been thinking about is this identity piece.

I keep thinking about how I was planning my future from my past experiences, when what seems to be true is that something is coming out of this experiment and experience, which is nothing I've ever done before. I keep thinking that maybe I need to release more of the me I've known myself to be in order to make room for the me that's trying to emerge. I don't think I'm necessarily losing one to the other. It feels like I'm simply making room for the other.

I came to Alaska to be a part of all these projects, and It's been very interesting to see how many have stalled. I do need to make some decisions about what to do next. I do have these irreconcilable distances between New Jersey and Alaska, but I want to get beyond that and get to the heart of the matter. So that's what I've been doing. I'm trying to reduce the stimuli and listen to my heart. There could not be a better geographical place for the heart than Alaska. She is stunning and majestic and sacred. On a night like tonight, when the sun is going down and the moon is coming up at the same time, it's unlike any other place on earth.

Day 17: Come On Up for the Rising

WOW. Things are starting to accelerate. I was watching some of Kyle's videos last night, and I took notes about what I wanted to talk about today: I want to move to a place where the question, "What do I do?" leaves my vocabulary. That lit me up! I got excited about living a life where my confidence and sense of knowing comes from within. We have been taken out of ourselves. We've been trained to believe that the people and the systems outside of us know better than our own sense of things, and I want out of that.

In my work as a spiritual educator, I tell people, "I don't have your answers," Yet, I definitely went to L.A. wanting Kyle to give me the answers. What a paradox! And that desire definitely caused me pain. Over the last two weeks I've been staying present with the pain and it's been breaking down and – ultimately – breaking away the core of who I am. It's necessary in order to live from my heart. To do so, I have to stop living from my mind. I can see that all that I've been has gotten me to this moment – all of the ways I've thought, all of the ways I've lived, all of the decisions I've made, all the ways in which I've expressed who I am – all of it has gotten me to this moment: meditating and then recording with a shaking cell phone. But it's not necessarily what's going to get me to the next moment, and THAT is more powerful today than it was a couple of weeks ago.

This experiment has been downright frightening. It's felt like death because, on some level, it is death. And isn't it purposeful and perfect that Easter is on the horizon? I'm not a practicing Catholic, but I grew up Catholic, and I have great appreciation for the symbolism of some of the holy days. The metaphysical interpretation of Easter is very powerful. For me, the resur-rection shows us that they can kill you but they cannot take your life. You cannot kill energy. We are eternal. We are made up of stardust.

Last night my friend, Kelly and I drove south of Anchorage to watch the full moon rise. It had already come up over the Chugach mountains that line the city and we went to a place called Potter Marsh where the moon had not yet climbed above the peaks. I was watching the white glow prior to the moon's sliver appearing, and was impressed by how bright the light was before we could actually see the source. I looked up at the stars and the planets and was thinking about how the Creator is so playful. It said to Itself, "I'm going to be looking through these expressions of myself called people, and we're going to be looking skyward, so let me put myself in actual shapes and sizes that we can name and label. The Big Dipper, Orion. It will be a playground above us."

Nothing matters, and everything matters. You hang out in the darkness with the moon rising and the planets twinkling, and everything becomes really, super clear. The Intelligence that's raising that moon is rising in me. I am here to give it full permission to guide me. It does have my answers. It is my clarity. All that I am looking for, I already have. I've known this, but clearly I have to become aware of how I've allowed my thoughts to live for me and to compress, restrict, and oppress me. I'm just in awe of how it all is evolving. I'm awake for it, I'm aware of it, I'm staying present with it, and these hour-long meditations are absolutely the perfect prescription for me right here and right now.

Day 18: It's Within

I'm really excited today because I'm going to do some heart-work exercises from the Flow Group. I'm going to write down all the decisions I believe I have to make. I'm going to list all of the possible paths I could choose in regard to these decisions and list my responses to them. Then I'll put each decision in my body. I'm going to feel each one and take note of what constricts me and what expands me. I'm going to trust that the expansive response is coming from my heart and that, by saying yes and trusting, everything I need to know next will appear.

The other exercise is to make a list of my heart's desires – all of the things I really want to be, all the things I want to do and experience – from the point of view that I can't fail, I won't get punished, I won't go broke, and my life won't go irretrievably off-course. Then I'm going to take one thing from the list, and I'm going to DO one of those things today. I'm taking a leap of faith, and I'm taking all of my decision-making into my body and allowing my inner guidance system and my heart to tell me which way to go. Why not give that a try with me?

Day 19: Feel the Fear and Do It Anyway

Last night, I was on the phone with Sacha and I realized what a great gift it is to have somebody hold me accountable. It's a great gift to have someone who knows my dreams and visions and knows what's going on for me because she's going through it, too. We were talking about these post-meditation videos and she was telling me that she cross-promotes them from her business and personal pages. I told her I was just posting my videos on the This Awakening Spirit page. She asked me, "Why aren't you putting this on your personal page?" I knew the answer, but I didn't want to say it. She intuitively asked, "Are you scared?" And of course, it all came rushing to the surface: "Hell yeah, I'm scared!"

I got a chance to talk about that with her and make room for the part of me that was feeling way too vulnerable about being rejected and made fun of, which goes back to my childhood (perhaps you can relate.) I felt afraid to show my authentic self on my personal Facebook page where people actually know me. To be so raw in front of them felt like a big deal.

Sacha said, "But Camille, how are you going to reach thousands of people if you're not being real and authentic to the ones that already know you?" She had a point. After we hung up, I shared the Day 2 video on my personal page. It felt exciting and scary...and tremendously liberating. I was no longer giving power to fear. I thought about the exercises I did yesterday, where I made a list of things that light me up: Being with my friends. Getting on my bicycle. Going to the beach. Then it became universal. It excites me to explore a new radio show format. It excites me to get up on stage and do exploratory conversations with people. It excites me to be impactful. It excites me to work with a group of people toward something that goes beyond myself. I was giving my heart a chance to speak. And, true to my word, I did one of the things on my list – something I've been talking about doing for a long time. I recorded a video asking Bruce Springsteen for an interview. It felt incredible. To see myself ask for the interview, I was like YES. Absolutely. That got me thinking, what else can I do from my list? This feels like a good way to start living from my heart.

I looked over the other list, where I wrote down the decisions I believe I have to make. I had so many that I had to put it down and come back to it, because – dang! It was quite the list of things that are weighing me down. Questions like: Should I stay in Alaska or go back to New Jersey? Should I go back to New Jersey for May and then go to L.A. for the Agape meditation retreat and then come back up here? Should I drive my car up here and leave it, or....Hold on! All of that is an obsession with not knowing. Behind that is an obsession with asking questions that posture me as not knowing. And behind THAT is part of me that has bought into looking for answers outside of myself and believing that I don't have the answer.

When I spent a pile of money to take courses to learn how to do all the things that entrepreneurs are doing to sell their services and products, it was what I thought I had to do. I'm glad I did it, because I did learn many things. But this whole idea of grabbing emails and creating funnels and getting the subject and the wording just so, all designed to get people to open my emails – it felt wrong from the beginning. It felt laborious and against my authentic self. Behind all of that effort were all of these "what ifs."

What if they don't open the email?

What if I don't word this correctly?

What if, what if, what if?

This just isn't my truth. I'm doing something different, and I'm starting to touch what it is that I'm here to do.

Day 20: Beyond the Headlines

I needed a few minutes after meditation this morning because I'm not quite sure where I traveled to. Holy Toledo! It's a very odd sensation when time and space and your place in them go away. I set the clock for an hour, got myself settled into the embrace of the well-worn couch...and the next thing I know, the alarm went off. I didn't sleep, I was just...somewhere. It was a place without any problems. It was without any headlines or questions. It was without anything material. It was just all a suspended state of peace and lightness and quiet.

When I got ready to record after today's meditation, my mind said to me, *You know, these videos remind me of when we did talk radio.* When I went from DJing FM music to hosting AM talk radio, I was petrified. Yes, I was on my creative edge, but it was immensely stressful. I had to sound smart and knowledgeable in real time with no do-overs. I had to know what I was talking about. I had to have enough content to fill the time if I didn't get any callers. I was no longer able to use music or my history with it to fill dead air. To say I felt nauseous is an understatement. I don't feel that level of stress or nausea now, but it's no mistake that my mind made that association. It sprang up as I was thinking, *What do I really have to offer?* I was conscious today of feeling the need to do something well, to do something right or perfect, to make this video mean something.

Perhaps that's normal. Perhaps that's yet another extension of the mind. Thank goodness I know other people who are doing this. Every now and then we check in with each other: "What the hell did we say yes to?" This experiment is fascinating, among other things. I'm seeing how daily meditation sets me up for the rest of the day, calling in the flashes of insight and under-standing.

Day 21: She is Risen

For many people it's Easter Sunday. For me, it's my own Resur-rection Day. I had an interesting dream this morning. I was in an audience, and there was a guy with grey hair and a beard sitting unusually high above me; sitting next to him was Oprah Winfrey. He was talking to her and calling her the master teach-er and asking her all these questions: "How do I.... How do we...."

I got more and more upset. I turned to the person next to me and said, "I can't believe he keeps talking to her as if she knows more than we do about ourselves. He's acting as if we don't have our own answers." As the dream went on, I went off on the guy, saying, "What are you doing? You're giving Oprah more power than is her own. You're making everybody believe that they have to go outside of themselves to know what their truth is!" And then I woke up. Wow. OK, got it. I value Oprah and what she shares, but I was so clear about the importance of knowing my own truth.

After dreaming and meditating, I went to my spiritual center, ACSL, where I get to be of service to others, and today I was inspired to go into the little kid's area to see if they needed some help. There were a lot of little kids there, so they asked me to stay on. I saw a little boy sitting on a chair crying and having a tough time and I was immediately drawn to him. I sat down in the tiny chair next to his and asked how he was doing, and he just kept crying. So, I got him tissues and I put my hand on his back and did a little Reiki love. He leaned a little closer to me and I got a little closer to him, and eventually just put him on my lap. Soon after, I felt wetness coming down my legs.

I realized what was happening and I scooped him up to take him into the restroom. He propped himself up on the toilet and, as soon as he was able to do the job properly, he got a big smile on his face and started giggling. The joy he displayed, after having his needs met, was amazing.

The house I am housesitting at is very close by, so I got him some loaner pants from the lost and found and took his clothes home and dried them. I didn't want him to be uncomfortable or embarrassed. I got back just before the kids walked out to join the adults at the end of the service; he and I walk out hand in hand and sat together on the edge of the stage, and he leaned completely into me. That little boy taught me that we all have that little child within us, and it needs to be acknowledged. I certainly have been face to face and heart to heart with my little girl these past several weeks now. That little boy just needed to be loved. He needed to be comforted and to be told that everything was OK and he was safe. That's what I told him – he was safe and loved.

I would imagine it's something that you might begin to do for yourself, if you haven't been doing it already. The way we talk to ourselves, to the child within us, is important. It would not have been appropriate for me to tell this little boy, "Get over it! Stop crying." or any of the harsh things I've been saying to myself. To be held, to have somebody there who cares; we all need that at times.

Day 22: If at First You Don't Succeed

It's 5:00 in the afternoon. I don't know what to say...I didn't do well this morning. I couldn't get up. This 7:00 am thing is really a challenge for me and I'm not sure what I need to do about that. I'm not sure if I need to make it a little bit later so I actually have success. I'm not sure if there's something going on personally with my health that's making me unable to get up in the morning. I got some writing done, but all I can say is that I don't feel good about the meditation piece today. This is not about me feeling bad; it's about me figuring out what I need to do to make this habit stick.

Day 23: The $400 Lesson

This morning went much better than yesterday. The alarm went off at 7:00, I got up, splashed some water on my face, made myself a cup of coffee, and got into my meditation by about 7:25. And by that I mean, I sat my ass on that couch and closed my eyes. That's a good thing. I came to my meditation hoping for some reprieve from the action-packed motion picture that is my mind. Instead, the movie rolled on across the screen of my mind and I just watched it. When I found myself getting frustrated that I wasn't going someplace deeper, I just took a deep breath and let it go, detached from what my mind was fussing over.

Yesterday was an interesting day; I got to see a mechanism of my thinking that I'm now releasing. I call it the $400 lesson learned. Soon after I got to Alaska in February, someone asked me to emcee an event on April 22nd. At the time I said, "I can't say yes because I don't know if I'm going to be here." If I'd said yes, I would've had a decent paying gig and money to pay some bills AND my future plans would have actually bent around what I scheduled. I would've been creating my future instead of waiting for it to happen to me.

However, I said no to that gig because I thought there would be something else that was coming that was more in alignment with my desires. I thought that saying yes to the first gig would have blocked me from other opportunities. That's definitely a pattern I've had. I've been afraid to make decisions – not only because I've been thinking they're the wrong decisions, but I've also worried that certain decisions are somehow outside of the path I'm on and all that I'm yearning to experience and call forth. The truth is, I understand that whatever comes into my path IS my path. Had I said yes to the first gig, I would've known I would've been here until April 22nd. Consequently, I could've filled my time with other things.

So, I decided to fly back to New Jersey to be with my mom for the month of May. Right after I booked my ticket, I got a call from my friend, Loren wanting me to do some radio work in Alaska...starting the exact day that I head East. OK, pause. The victim response to this would be, "Why can't I get a break?" But I know that's not true. What did I have to do as I was thinking through this? I had to love myself like the little boy I talked about on Sunday. I had to hold myself mentally and emotionally. I had to be really gentle with myself because the harsh inner critic was ready to take me down on this. I thought, *Nope. I'm not doing that.* This is an abundant universe. I can't be attached to how each day is, because each day just IS. And for this, I'm very, very grateful.

Day 24: Silence is Golden

I woke up at 6:00 am to participate in a weekly call with my beloved soul brother, spiritual colleague, and friend of more than 20 years, Kaleem. Every Wednesday morning, we support each other by listening deeply and by using what we call Affirmative Prayer.

I grew up with prayer couched in begging and beseeching. It was about praying to a power outside of myself that had good days and not so good days; you had to approach carefully. I always wondered if I was worthy of having my prayers answered. These days, my prayerful life is happening all the time and I understand that the word is creative whenever it's used. This is a great gift that we've been given by the Creator. Our word is creative. We are immersed in universal laws that are constantly creating and when you understand and work in alignment with this, you release your victimhood and become a conscious co-creator of your everyday experience.

Kaleem and I were also talking about this event that we've been working on for quite some time, now. We've been inspired to do a spiritual response to President Trump. I'm sharing this with you because, after our prayer call, I took our conversation in to meditation. This morning I realize that – more often than not – I'm in an exploratory state. I'm really excited to be involved with Kaleem who, along with me, has been willing to remain open, flexible, and available to whatever is trying to express through us.

The content and our presentation of it has been morphing every day that we talk. We are still in the exploratory phase of the title, alone; I've gotten passionate feedback from all political sides about the title. A lot of people are drawing conclusions before they even hear what the content is. At the same time, it's a little scary – as in, mysterious – because we don't really know all that it's going to be. We know pieces of it. We just decided to go forward and open the door and begin and see what happens.

I'm finding that the phrase "silence is golden" is something I'm relating to today. There's something about the silence that's calling me in. I want to go someplace without a lot of stimuli, do some writing, and just empty out. Things have been percolating and rearranging within, and now they're presenting to me anew. I want to cast a net and pull in as much as I can before it goes away. Perhaps this quiet time is necessary so that I can feel into the feedback I've been getting. At the core of this Spiritual Response presentation, I don't want us to suffer so much. We're suffering in many ways, whether we're young people or old or in between. We have an opportunity to stop fighting, to listen to each other and to respect each other and seek a common ground. That's what inspires me.

I get to practice what I want to teach. Can I listen deeply? Can I respect another's opinions even though they firmly disagree with my own? I know that, to be called out to do something like this, I'm called in to myself. If I'm going to be part of this presentation, it's important for me to come from a place of being centered. These meditations are helping me find that place and stay connected to it throughout the day.

Day 25: I Need to Know

Today I witnessed the barrage of my thoughts for almost the entire 60 minutes of meditation. In the midst of that I was thinking about two things.

One is this revelation I had about how I make decisions and, more specifically, how I don't make decisions, based on thinking that the situation is somehow not in alignment with my greatest good. I've been looking back over the last couple of years with gentle observation, seeing how that has played out. I feel that this insight is a new, important filter to apply as I go forward.

The other thing is that I feel like I'm walking through a valley in the desert, and I don't necessarily like this. I know there is value in the valley and all of that. However, it's a very uncomfortable time. I don't like not knowing; it's just a true thing to say out loud today. I would much prefer a very clear and definitive knowing of what I'm doing. I would prefer having a booked calendar for the rest of the year, filled with the activities that light me up: radio work, speaking around the state and the country, women's workshops and events, teaching spiritual education classes.

And yet, I have nothing on my calendar. There's a major pause going on and I don't like it. I'm not forging ahead, being in "the doing". I'm not sure what's mine to do with all of this. I don't like being a not-sure woman with gifts and talents and a lot of ideas about what to do with them, but no real sense of where to direct them. And yet, here I am: Day 25, getting ready to go back to New Jersey next weekend. I feel like I have to put something in place and yet, I know that that forcing something just to make my mind more comfortable won't work.

I know that it's a luxury that I can spend this much time with myself, doing this deep work. I'm taking a fine-tooth comb through everything: radio work, voice work, speaking, facilitating workshops, and teaching. I'm allowing myself to feel anew, with each and every thing - what lights me up? What do I want to do? And then I give myself permission to simply say yes to those things and allow my heart to show me the way.

I know that I want to help people. I know that I need to live a purposeful and meaningful life. I want to be a part of a bigger solution, and it feels very uncomfortable to feel this far away from activity. I can see a big part of me is afraid "it's" over or "it's" not going to happen. It's afraid that the whole dream is a bust. I need to sit with and love that part of myself, because that fear has been around me for quite some time. There's a lot of deconstruction going on, and I love it.

Day 26: The One Behind the Thoughts

Discipline is an interesting thing. I have an opportunity to master the discipline of this experiment. Though I meditated this morning, it's already 8:00 pm and I'm just getting to the video. I'm a night person (opinion) who's almost always had late jobs (fact) and I feel like this impacts what I'm doing. I'm rewriting most of my story these days, and this is one piece of it.

In meditation, I felt connected to the One behind the thoughts. It revealed that I can look beyond what I normally see. In other words, when I looked beyond speaking and radio and all of that, it showed me that I have so much possibility. I'm curating an anthology about daughters caring for their moms—honest snapshots about the experience. The submissions are crazy, wonderful, poignant, and sad. If you're a daughter caring for your mom, you'll feel understood. If you're not, you'll be able to tap into an amazing, rich experience that many of us are going through.

The other piece that came up is my rock 'n roll radio podcast, The Camille Conte Show. I'm in my 5th year of creating this commercial-free, listener-supported radio show, and just surpassed 25,000 downloads! My mind has been looking through a specific filter where things must be a specific way to be considered "successful" or "meaningful". And when they're not, my mind interprets this as failure. It's measuring what I've lost or am about to lose. I'm excited – understanding this will help me with all that is happening within and through me.

I sat with the One behind the thoughts today, and what It had to say was important.

Day 27: "Transformation Sucks," said the Caterpillar

The Universe gave me an important message at a friend's house today. I noticed a quote on her wall: "The greatest gift you have to give is that of your own self-transformation. Period". That is amazing because I've been thinking about whether or not it's appropriate for me to be spending my time with/ focused on my own transformation. Have you ever felt this way?

Usually I go through personal growth privately or with close friends. I don't know that the caterpillar announces to the world, "Hey! I'm dying and rearranging my organs and turning into soup, so I can become a butterfly!" I'm pretty sure we like the butterfly OR the caterpillar, not the moments in between. And yet, those moments are crucial and universal. We've all lived some form of that transformative process, where we're dying to who we've been and becoming what we are to be.

When I saw that cloth at my friend's house, it was a reminder. The Universe was telling me, "Camille...keep going. Keep going. Yes, you're making these videos that you don't like most of the time and – four days in a row – you've put them off until the end of the day to rebel against this whole morning thing. And just keep doing them."

There's something about shining the light on the whole trans-formation process, a process which is ultimately beautiful. But before it's beautiful, it's messy, scary, and feels a lot like death...because it is. But it doesn't have to take place in darkness.

Day 28: Kindness Matters

The theme today is kindness and taking responsibility for words and the tone used to deliver those words - how we think about people in our minds, how we feel about people in our hearts, and what kind of energy infuses our actions.

Sometimes kindness requires us to take the high road when we want to take the low road. Kindness is about letting go of grudges, being the first to apologize, and the first to forgive. Kindness is about seeking to be of service.

I went back to the Alaska Center for Spiritual Living this morning, my spiritual home, and I hung out with the 7 to 11-year-olds this time. We were talking about change and how the only thing you can really change is how you look at and think about things. It was remarkable to me how many of these young people had stories about being bullied. The youngest, who was 7, talked about a school bully. I asked her how she handled that, and she said, "I thought about it and I decided it was best to walk away."

How remarkable and hopeful that such a young person was able to understand, in that moment, that the kind way, the high road way, was to simply walk away. To not meet the bully's energy with her own bully energy, to not further engage or push. Once again, I'm touched by the children. I'm mindful that, in five days, I'm getting on a plane again and flying across the country to New Jersey to be of service to my mom. Rather than struggle or fight, I can trust and know that, within this, are the seeds of what is mine to do.

Day 29: Refusal and Then Surrender

Truth: there is a me that does not want to do this Confusion Experiment. She has been resisting and putting up a fight from the very beginning. It's the me that's says, *You know what? We're not doing this anymore. We're not showing our face, talking about our most vulnerable experience and reality. NO.* On some level, I relate to what she's talking about. And…I gave my word. Without your word, what do you have? I have to keep my word to myself.

Yesterday I saw a man standing on the street corner with a little sign that said, "US Army Vet." He was wearing a ball cap and, as I was waiting for the light to change, I saw him take his cap off. He ran his hand through his hair. There was something about that gesture that opened my heart. I was thinking about how difficult it must be to stand on a corner and ask for help. I decided to offer him some cash. He had been drinking; I could smell the alcohol when I rolled down the window, but it didn't matter. The smile that came across his face was precious – the look of a person who is seen and responded to as a human being.

Later in the evening, I was sharing food and company with some friends. One friend is very upset with what's happening in our country. He was so angry, concerned, and fearful – almost obsessed. His wife and I listened as he shared his feelings. When he finished I asked, "To what end? All of this energy and passion – to what end? At some point we have to consider being our own version of an answer to all of this. You're reacting and responding to what is already done. Headlines have been written. The best we can do now is to ask, "What is mine to do? How can I bring my passion, skills, and talents to this experience in a way that is meaningful?"

Look, the situation already is. To keep using our precious moments, now and yet to be, by responding to something that's already done is a waste of our valuable time. That's where I am as I move forward with preparations for my collaborative talk about responding spiritually to President Trump. I'm wondering if this talk is even mine to do; I know a conversation is yet to be had about that. I'm just allowing myself to know that I am in my divine plan. There's nothing outside of me that I have to get. Everything is right where I am, and that's a good thing.

Day 30: I'll Take Instinct Over Experience Any Day

Day 30! I can definitively say that things have changed since Day 1 in California. I feel like I have a headlamp on and I've been rummaging around, finding interesting artifacts from my own thinking. As I continue to meditate for an hour in the morning, I notice that my insights are coming later in the day. I'm definitely having these moments where, suddenly, I'm seeing something from an observer's perspective, looking at a pattern of my thinking.

Yesterday evening I realized that I've had a belief that says knowing is important. Knowing is success. Then the belief became a value. Or maybe it started as a value and then became a belief – that's not important. What's important is the revelation about this idea that says knowing is the best. Knowing what you're doing, where you're going, and how you're getting there is the way to succeed. It makes tremendous sense to me that I have had these moments of sheer terror when I don't have a succinct, detailed plan of where it is that I'm going. This is helpful as I continue my goal of moving from "knowing" (being in my mind), into my heart and my body.

When I left Alaska on October 28th of 2013, I knew a handful of things. I knew I was safe. I knew I had a car and insurance and AAA. I knew I had a specific amount of cash to seed this sabbatical adventure I'm on. But outside of that, I was relying on my instinct because I had no experience with what I was about to do. As time has gone on and things have happened and fallen away, this belief about needing to know has emerged more obviously. It's caused me to experience stress and, ironically, to be distant from the very thing that belief says I should have. Today – at least right now – I don't need to know because there is a Knower within me. I've sensed and relied on this for some time, but there have also been subconscious beliefs blocking a greater relationship with the Knower. In this meditative experience, I'm finding revelation and, ultimately, release.

When I first started this experiment, I was wrapped around my thoughts and identifying as the struggle. Today is a different experience. Today I'm able to observe my thoughts as they float across the screen of the mind. I'm better at recognizing when I've attached myself to something, and I have the awareness and tools to sit with that or change it, if need be. Today, I don't need to know.

Day 31: A Spiritual Response to President Trump

Today all attention is on tonight's webinar: A Spiritual Response to President Trump. I've spoken about this in previous videos. It's been a powerful, interesting and often times frustrating experience with my beloved friend Kaleem. When I begin working in collaboration with someone, especially a friend and a colleague that I've known forever, all is new. It requires a lot of give and take and it's been fascinating to see us both give up a lot of preferences to find common ground that allows us to move forward with the vision that we both have. I realized that this is exactly what we're going to talk about tonight: finding and working from common ground and allowing everything else to just be what it is.

The other focus is a question I encourage us all to ask: "Do I want to use my precious "Now" energy that is coming through me in this very moment to get emotionally wrapped around the axle of something that's already over and done with?" This is part of the paradigm shift and mental shift that I want to bring to our discussion. I'm in the process of doing this, myself. I have in no way mastered this, but I'm aware of it and I'm working with it. Am I reacting and responding to what's already done (in any area of my life), or am I choosing to use the creative, fresh energy coming through to be part of a solution?

I've been going through a lot of interesting awakenings as part of these meditations. One big awakening has been around looking to the future through the lens of the past: what I've done, how I've done it, and who I've been. Looking through that to measure my success, coupled with a deep-seated belief that knowing is the formula to success, creates the mental chaos that I have been experiencing. If I believe that knowing equals success, then I have evidence that I'm a failure when I don't know...or so this belief tells me.

Looking through these filters has caused me to be blind to something new that's now in the picture like this webinar, the anthology of daughters caring for mothers. I can do the things I've loved and known; radio, speaking, teaching. However, I'm also opening up space and allowing other things to come into my sight that have never happened before. The outdated filters show that nothing's happening in my life. When I remove them, that statement is clearly untrue.

Day 32: No Woman, No Cry

In the last 20 minutes of meditation, the floodgates opened. I used to put a lot of energy into stressing about how much I cry, mostly because of people's opinions or comments about it. By the time I turned 50 and my hormones went through their rage in the cage, I just began to love myself in a deep way. It doesn't matter whether that was a result of hormones or (more likely) about opening my heart. I accept it. I accept me.

I'm feeling emotional about leaving for New Jersey on Saturday; it's never easy for my heart to leave these two places. Considering how often I've left Alaska for Jersey and vice versa, you would think this would be easy but it's not. I have beautiful people here who are so generous to me. Give thanks for the people in your life that give to you, whether it's with their love or support or time. We need each other. I couldn't live this crazy, off-the-shelf life if it wasn't for my dear friends who put a roof over my head, who put food in my belly, who love me and comfort me, who hug and listen to me.

Now, I'll be going back to my mom's house, and she will love me and feed me, and I will do the same for her. I am looking forward to going back to New Jersey and connecting with her, interestingly. That's not always the case. Maybe it's because the energy for this Alaska trip has been so discombobulated. I know that's because I have gone through and continue to go through such a major deconstruction of the self.

I was thinking about that during my meditation. For anyone who thinks that meditation is about NOT thinking, let me tell you – that's not the meditation I know. For me, an hour of meditation is mostly 58 minutes of my thoughts freaking out across the screen of my mind. My thoughts, your thoughts, everybody's thoughts – they're all there! It's like, what the hell? Who makes these? When does the manufacturing process slow down?

Now I don't even remember what I was thinking because more thoughts took my attention away.

My friend and I did our webinar – A Spiritual Response to President Trump. I'm so proud of us. Our friendship took a tender turn at one point preparing for this, but we were inspired to stay with it for almost three months until it happened. We needed to empty ourselves of ourselves, do you know what I'm saying? For my friend, speaking in front of a live, online audience was a huge stretch. He just kept letting go of his preferences and limiting thoughts. We both did. I'm so proud of us for doing that. Now we'll just see what we're inspired to do next.

Irreconcilable distances is the crux of my feeling-state today as I prepare myself to say goodbye to friends and to this beautiful place. I know it's not forever, so why all of the "drama"? That comment right there is coming from outside of me and reminds me: Don't be harsh and rough to the tender child within you. Don't be harsh and rough to the sweet presence that, too often, we dismiss and chastise: "Get over yourself." The child inside of us wants to be part of our everyday living. We need their sweetness and their innocence, their wisdom. If more of us brought that little girl or little boy out into our expression, things would be different. I look at Donald Trump and I see a little boy that's still trying to get love, attention, and approval. I mean, my gosh. I've never seen a public figure like this, so desperate for approval, desperate to be seen. When you look at it through the eyes of compassion and empathy, it's like wow – we've got to pray for everybody and affirm that there's something great and magnificent unleashing itself through each and every one of us.

Lastly, Sacha, Mark, Kat and I had our first follow-up video phone call yesterday. I've got to say, the theme of the check-in was that everybody's a bit fucked up! So, OK. Alright. When we left after our weekend together, something had happened that we've never been able to put back together again. When you've had a major internal deconstruction and your pieces and parts are strewn across the floor (and somebody burned the instruction sheet), you're like, what the hell? You try to put things back together, but you realize pieces are missing and you don't even know if the parts that are left fit together anymore.

This is the proverbial clearing of the table and starting over. You're waiting for parts to be delivered because you know you're putting something completely new together. So what do you do while you're waiting? Meditate, I guess. Maybe I'll find the instructions there.

Day 33: What the Fuck is Going On?

You know, I have to be honest. Today is one of those days where I just want to stay under the covers. I don't want to talk to anybody, I don't want to see anybody. And that's mostly because, last night, I had an unexpected breakdown/meltdown. A big chunk had to be released last night.

I was at the end of a long day, just sitting in the dark, thinking back over these last few wild months. The thing that probably brought me to my knees was remembering how joyful I was going into that L.A. weekend. I have not fully felt joy to that degree since I got back. I was remembering how, after I had my own meltdown in front of the Flow Group, things seemed to get worse from there.

Now I'm thinking, was it worse? Is it worse? I don't want to label these experiences in any negative way because really, it's just what is. The mind tries to label based on what it thinks is happening, and all sorts of feelings follow those conclusions, but overall I'm sitting here feeling really sunk. I'm going back to Jersey with this measuring stick that hasn't been able to measure a whole lot since I got to Anchorage. I came out of a spinning situation in Jersey. Then I came into a spinning situation in Alaska. I was scrambling to put work together, and then canceled the women's retreat because I got selected for Kyle's retreat, and here I am, 30-something days later thinking, *I'm going back to New Jersey with what*?

I know what I'm going back with. I'm going back with myself, with more awareness, and with a focus on two books. But still – it's been a weird two months. Alaska is rarely like this. Usually I come back to Alaska and things get lined up and are in the flow. Looking back though, I think: Were there advances? Were there successes? What did I get done? All of that stuff that comes from my mind. When I measure what simply is against that, it's all loss. And all loss feels crappy. So I don't feel too great right now. I know I'll have a vibrational shift after I do my gratitude work and call forth what I want to experience today. I have the tools that can make that happen.

So, yes, something huge unleashed last night. I asked the Universe, "What's here for me to understand?" It feels like there's more here and – for right now – I'm tired of this self-analytical transformational work. I truly don't know how the caterpillar does it. I think the butterfly's got the easy part.

Day 34: Yesterday Doesn't Exist

The time-space continuum rolls on. I am in New Jersey, in the bedroom where I grew up, with the psychedelic wallpaper that was much more enjoyable in the 70s (I was stoned most of the time) and I already feel out of it. Every time I make my way from one side of the country to the other, it takes time to reboot. I'm crossing four time zones, but also moving from one life to another. So yesterday didn't exist. I didn't meditate or make a video.

Again, after 30-something days of meditation, the quantity of thoughts has not subsided at all. Today my mind was reminding me of all the things that I have to do and all the things I'm not doing and all the things I didn't do. It's doing an excellent job of laying it all out: my entire existence, every nook and cranny. Just in case I was unaware of my "failure", my mind is being sure to show me all this and to give its opinion every once in a while.

My mom, who is 86, is doing a really great job of living her life. And she's still in this home and there are a lot of things that she can't do anymore. I have no shortage of physical labor in front of me, and I'm looking forward to working up a sweat and helping her get ready for the next season, another hot summer. My mind is creating quite the to-do list. Of course, my body's saying, you might want to give us a day or two to get back into the skin of things. I'm still in Alaska, even though I'm here in New Jersey.

And yet, I could not wait to get into my meditation today. I was really looking forward to the stillness and being with myself in that deep way. It's wonderful to know this is something I enjoy and look forward to. I need to keep myself centered during these times of far-reaching change.

Day 35: All I Have is My Word

I got this Facebook message from a friend: "Hi, I'm not exactly sure what's going on. I listened to your radio show and you talked about being in a vacuum. Where are you? What's happening?" These are all excellent questions.

It's late here in New Jersey, and what I realized is that I spent all this time making it OK to not meditate and do this video. The

Camille that successfully put it off is the Camille that blissfully falls away in meditation, but she still doesn't like doing these videos. (In my head, she just corrected me, "stupid videos,") I was getting ready for bed, feeling so tired, and then realized – wait a minute. Whether I think these videos are stupid or not, I gave my word to myself, to Kyle, and to the group that I was going to meditate from 7:00-8:00 am every morning and roll a video afterwards. I have been watching how easily those commitments can erode. What (and who) causes them to erode? What did I give power to today and all those other days when I didn't meditate at 7:00 am, and instead meditated later in the evening? What voice is telling me that it's OK to miss today? It's not OK. So here it is, nearly 11:00 pm, and I'm in front of my phone's camera. I'm going to try again tomorrow to get back into alignment with my word and what I said I was going to do, and not let these other voices take hold.

It has been a bumpy ride, though, and being here makes it challenging to find my footing. The last thing I want to do is sit in front of the mirror of my post-meditation video while the stressors of being a caregiver reach for me. This is an incredibly humbling experience that includes some shame over the way I sometimes lose patience with my mom. On top of that, there is living grief around the loss of the mom I once had, even though she's still alive and well. But it's all projected loss, compounded with the loss of my own sense of what I'm doing with my life, the loss of my own sense of clarity.

In this bedroom, I think about young Camille's dreams, how she saw the life ahead of her, and how life has unfolded since then. I think about that line in Springsteen's song, "Is a dream alive that don't come true, or is it something worse?" I feel like I've got to get a handle on things. I've got to focus back in because it's felt incredibly uncomfortable wandering the streets of my own consciousness, trying to figure out what the fuck is going on.

Meanwhile, the whole world is having its own problems while I'm pretending I've got problems. I don't have any problems!

I have no problems whatsoever! It's the most bizarre experiment I've ever been inside of. Tomorrow, something must change. I must change. All of this has got to change, even if it's just by a small degree, tomorrow.

Day 36: I am the I Am, and So are You

Wednesdays are a really great day. For the last three years I've had my weekly prayer phone call with soul brother, Kaleem. Though we're now four time zones apart, today we had another wonderful, prayerful hour together. He held space for me as I unload this story one last time. I don't want to keep telling this story inside or outside of myself, and yet I feel like it needed some attention from someone I really admire and has known me for many years. Kaleem was able to remind me of some very important things. He mentioned a quote from Peter Deunov: "Do not look for happiness outside yourself. The awakened seek happiness inside."

That's my journey, the one that kicked off 2017, the one I wanted to help other people to take – the inward journey. How humbling that I have to take the journey, over and over, before helping others who want to seek within. And, nothing resets my mind and renews my story better than my spiritual practices. It might be affirmative prayer where I'm speaking with positive certainty about the conditions and situations of my life, or it might be meditating. Whatever it is, keep going through it.

Kaleem and I were talking about the caterpillar, the transformational process in the chrysalis, and the butterfly. It is powerful to surrender to transformation. I've certainly been resisting it. I am fluent in the language of resistance and I've been speaking it for days now. This morning felt a bit more like surrender and acceptance of what is. This is another layer to shed, another layer of conditioning and thinking and internal infrastructures that no longer serve me. It's painful and frightening to bear witness to these infrastructures falling away.

Of course, as something falls away, the mind is desperate for something to immediately take its place, and that's not always what happens. There is a gooey, fluid process before the butterfly emerges. I am grateful for my time with my friend and for the things he reminded me of. I'm grateful to be in this home with my mom, taking care of her. I'm grateful for the roof over my head, the clothes on my back, the food in my belly, enough money to pay this month's bills, to be reunited with my car, my sister, and my nephews here in New Jersey. I'm maintaining an attitude of gratitude, and there is so much to be thankful for.

In fact, Kyle Cease is having his book launch at Barnes and Noble in New York City. I might hop on a bus and then a train to go say hi to him and give him a big hug and a thank you.

Kaleem shared another gem: "Anybody who puts the gift on the person outside of themselves is a fool." I understood that. It's not Kyle, it's not Kaleem, it's not the Michael Beckwith meditation retreat coming up at the end of this month. It's me. There's only one thing happening. We're all a reflection of ourselves and the other. That's the beauty of oneness. There's only one I, and I am the I AM, and so are you. May we find the courage, strength, and tenacity to continue to turn inward, toward The Thing that Knows.

Day 37: A Bus Driver Named Gina Perez

Last night I headed into New York City, taking the 167 bus into the Port Authority to go see Kyle Cease at his book launch.

As I got on, I was greeted by the bus driver, a woman named Gina Perez. For starters, Gina pointed out that I had dropped my glasses outside and I was able to grab those before we left which was great. I sat up front and watched Gina say hello to every passenger, welcoming them on the bus. A family was getting on the bus – child, mother, and a grandmother – and while the mother was taking care of the child, the grandmother was dealing with this large baby carriage. Gina goes outside and is talking to them, and the next thing I know she's helping them hoist this pretty cumbersome carriage onto the bus. She gives it its own seat right in front of mine and says, "Don't worry, we'll deal with payment in a bit. Let's just get going." Kindness in action.

At the next stop, there's an elderly gentleman in a wheelchair. Gina pulls up and opens the door. Once again, she goes outside and is talking to him, and I see her pointing to the bus. I see her attempting to close the wheelchair. I go outside to see how I can help; my motivation was to get us back on the road because I didn't want to be late. It was a selfish motivation that faded away pretty quickly.

This elderly man that we're helping is clearly living a rough life, and Gina treated him with unbelievable respect. The next thing I know, we're helping this gentleman get on the bus and Gina and I are closing up the wheelchair to try and get it on the bus, a bigger feat than the baby carriage she moved before. I'm waving to the passengers on the bus, thinking it would be nice to get a guy's help, but nobody came out! Gina said to me, "We don't need anybody's help. Let's show them what girl power is all about."

We close up the wheelchair and lift it onto the bus together. We figure out a way to secure it, and now I'm sitting next to the gentleman we just helped onto the bus. It was remarkable and inspiring to see the dignity with which Gina dealt with that passenger. We drive to his stop and Gina and I get the wheelchair off and help him down the steps while he thanked us. It was life changing for me. I spent the rest of the drive talking to this woman. I tell her, "You gotta win the Bus Driver of the Year award! You're amazing!" She says, "Oh my gosh, that's so kind of you. I've never won." As it turns out, there is such an award, and I will be nominating her for it.

All the way into the city, this woman inspired me deeply. She lives her life with focus and purpose: to be of service, to help every single passenger get to their destination safely, and to treat all people with dignity, respect and kindness. She talked about how she has to work twice as hard – all the women do –

because that's what it takes in a male dominated industry to prove that you're just as good as the guys and you deserve the same respect.

For all my worrying about being late, I realized we had no traffic. We were coming off the Turnpike and heading to the Lincoln Tunnel – that's always where there's traffic, with all the different roads merging - and there wasn't any! This had never happened. Gina and I were laughing – it was the traffic equivalent of the Red Sea being parted, such a reminder that we live in a benevolent universe and, when we are kind, kindness comes back to us. At the Port Authority, Gina took us to the end of the line to give us "VIP treatment". I've never had a bus driver do that before. A simple bus ride from Jersey to New York City became the most amazing teachable moment from the Universe.

Here's the point. We give away our power to other people – politicians, leaders, bosses, family, friends. It's time to take that power back and realize that you have power as you are. Your kindness, caring for others, treating others with respect and dignity and compassion – that's what it's all about. We have the opportunity to make a difference right now, today, in somebody's life, just like Gina Perez makes a difference every time she gets behind the wheel and drives that bus into the city.

I needed to be reminded that I have the power to make a difference right where I am. With my mom, with my family, with the neighbors on my block, and with every single person I come across. Join me. Let us make a difference. We may not be able to change the crumbling hierarchy from the top down, but we can build the new infrastructure from the bottom up so that – when the old system does come tumbling down – we're standing strong and moving on.

Because we've already called in the new way.

Day 38: Victory: Divide and Conquer or Unite and Uplift? We Decide.

I have a lot on my heart today. I'm grateful that I have my radio show because that's a place where I get to talk some things out with my audience. There is an incredible storm outside here in North Jersey, a torrential rain. I actually love rain storms because there's something really powerful about things washing away with the force of the rain. It's coming down hard and the wind is blowing, Mother Nature's way of transforming. She's going from winter into spring. It's a powerful reminder that Mother Nature is always showing me the ease and the flow and the change of life.

Yesterday I was watching a video from my beloved Sacha, and she just really poured her heart out. She was talking about contentment and whether or not it's a real thing. Are we supposed to feel content? She bravely and honestly said that she has everything that she needs, but still feels discontent. That is something I can definitely relate to. Sometimes we feel badly when talking about our discontent and wanting more.

I talk about wanting more from a place of gratitude. I make it a point every day to count the blessings that are overflowing in my life. And, let's not decide to believe that the spiritual journey means that we can't also feel this discontent. This is the divine nature. This is the creative energy of life that is constantly seeking an outlet. Even though we're grateful and can say, "Yes, I'm content," we can simultaneously say, "I also want more." I think that's one of the primary things about being centered in the heart. You can feel connected and still desire more because the Thing within us is constantly seeking an outlet.

The more you meditate, the more centered you get, and the more aware you get. And then, the more this discontent feeling rises to the surface, because that is our divine nature that is seeking to be expressed. I was really touched by Sacha's honesty and I'm thinking about it today as the rain is coming down heavily outside.

I'm also thinking about the old paradigm that is in our face right now as Americans: the definition of victory. Victory meaning, to divide and conquer. But I'm here to put the truth of my being forward, which is that victory means to unite and uplift. Divide and conquer is the old, patriarchal way of living. I'm not talking about men, per se, I'm talking about patriarchal and matriarchal, a template from which we have been living. Divide and conquer comes from the patriarchal way, while unite and uplift comes from the matriarchal way.

I am choosing to believe that the energy of dividing and conquering, which is so prevalent right now, is to have a reference point of what it is we truly want. For me, victory is about uniting ourselves with each other at that most basic, human level, and uplifting everybody. That's what I want; to uplift everyone with our gestures. This is not a playground, a place to work out unhealed little boy wounds. We can do so much more, and it's absolutely fascinating. And here's the other thing: you can't take down somebody's legacy. As my brilliant friend Janet said, "What they're really doing is creating their own legacy. And take a look at the actions that they're using to do it."

There is so much chaos and change going on in our country right now, and there's so much energy around leadership. For me personally, it is time to take back all of my leadership energy from whomever and whatever I've given it to. A path, a person, an organization, a political entity, a leader....no. I'm taking it all back.

This is the new paradigm – co-leadership. This is not about anybody doing my work. This is not about me electing somebody and then leaning back and either being happy with what they're doing or complaining. Co-leadership. Creating a world that works for each and every person, a perfect union. Not dismissing the weakest of us, but working with them, first. To first help our children, the elderly, the disenfranchised, the disabled. That is what this is about. My heart is full today. I'm kind of used to that. Thanks for listening.

Day 39: Empty

This is Day/Night 39. I didn't really have anything to say this morning, so I waited. I didn't have anything to say by mid-day or by this afternoon, so I waited some more. Here it is in the evening, and I still don't really have anything to say. I thought I'd roll tape and tell you that. I'm empty, and that's alright. It's actually a relief and a bit of a reprieve from all that has been thus far.

Day 40: Should I Stay or Should I Go?

I feel a lot of pressure today; I have to make a decision about where I'm spending my summer. I am split, 50/50, equal parts of me feeling I should be in New Jersey – no – in Alaska. I've already done the human pros and cons list, but I'm trying to move this into my body, so I can feel where I will thrive and what environment is going to serve me and what's going to help me resuscitate my financial life. But I do feel a lot of stress and pressure and I don't like how that feels.

I'm not exactly sure what to do about all of it. I know that, wherever I go, my good is there because I'm going to be there. I have a sister here and I have a sister in Alaska. My mom is here, but my friends are in Alaska. The mountains are in Alaska, but the concerts are in New Jersey. I guess it's a wonderful problem to have.

I think, underneath the pressure, I just feel that lingering disappointment that things haven't turned out the way I had hoped they would at this point. I'm having to keep accepting that disappointment and, hopefully, it will dissolve soon and be something else. Today I'm at my sister's, being of service to her and loving it, and tomorrow I go back and serve my mom. One of the challenges is balancing the service to myself. I'm hopeful that my meditation will help me ground into the answer of where to be this summer.

Day 41: Keep Your Eyes on the Vibrational Prize

I'm grateful for my spiritual practices. I'm grateful for an hour of meditation, and that when I go into it my mind still creates so much resistance. It's just funny! My mind still asks me, *Why are we doing this? It's such a long time.* It takes quite a while for that to settle down. I bring no expectations to this experience, none whatsoever. It is what it is.

This is why I use affirmative prayer because it helps my mind focus on what's real and true. Like someone said a long time ago, "With all thy getting, get thee understanding." In other words, understand how life works. Understand the spiritual behind the material. Understand the universal laws like gravity, the law of attraction, and the law of reciprocity. Understand how life works, and then work with it. This makes us co-creators of our own experience.

The illusion is that there are many things happening, but the truth is that this One Thing is so infinite and so unbounded, this One Thing is so intelligent, that it can make and create a variety of things. And yet, behind it all, there's only one thing happening. Affirmative prayer aligns you with that One Intelligence. And so I spoke the affirmative word for myself today: clarity is at hand. Unexpected good is at hand. I'm able to make the decisions I need for my life with ease and love and support, a sense of harmony and inner peace. Co-leadership. This is something that Kyle Cease said and Mr. Obama have talked about. This is the new paradigm. It's taking back our power from others; we're now waking up and understanding. We're finding the courage to dig deep, to sit in the stillness, to ask the question: what is mine to do? And then act from that inspiration.

I always find Mr. Obama's words to be of high vibration. He speaks with great eloquence and the energetic mold of his words is uplifting and keeps my eyes set on the prize, so to speak. We're here to love, we're here to help each other, we're here to support each other. I'm going to do that by smudging my sister's new house and asking all the spirits that have lived here to leave and create space for the new. I'm going to bless this home, get in my car, and head back to my mom's house and all that awaits me, knowing that I'm fully sourced, my needs are met, and I'm here to do what's mine to do.

Whatever's going on for you today, may you take the time to commune with Mother Nature and breathe. May you take the time to say a prayer for yourself and others and include your enemies or the ones you feel disconnected with. May you take the time to be still and give thanks. May you take the time to lend a helping hand.

Day 42: Keep Your Opinions to Yourself

I've got a lot in my head today. I had a relationship challenge prior to going into meditation, and during it, I was observing the thoughts and opinions that were going through my mind. Why did they do this or that? How come they didn't wait for this? How come they didn't wait for that? There was this amazing process of my mind putting a complete filter in front of my thinking as it relates to another person and the choices they made.

I grew up in a culture where everyone had opinions about everybody else. In fact, it was not uncommon for people to talk about other people and constantly give their opinions about what they were doing right or wrong and what they should or shouldn't do. I have found that I'm always very skeptical about sharing my intimate thoughts and feelings about the direction of my life because I don't necessarily want to hear people's opinions.

At the same time, I'm very conscious about giving opinions because it's been such a natural thing to do. I'm in a situation now where I have many opinions, but it's not appropriate for me to share them (I haven't been asked, for one thing). It can be hard to keep thoughts to ourselves sometimes. It may be difficult to witness the stress or the pressure that somebody is going through because of their choices, but in the end, what is it that I'm really here to do? I'm here to listen to that person and pray for them and be as compassionate as I can. I don't think I'm here to have an opinion, especially if I'm not asked. Because really, an opinion is just what somebody can say through their own experience, value system, and belief system.

Opinions about myself and things in my own life can be tricky, too. I just found this dry erase board where I had written my intentions for this year and all of the speaking and business goals, as well. Above it is the Flow Group questionnaire, the interview questions provided by Kyle Cease's team to guide the submission video I had to create. Looking back over the paperwork, I realized I had created some significant opinions about what was going to happen though none of it was really promised.

This is really about me forgiving myself. That's what I'm extending to myself today. I was so desperate for guidance and help. I felt exhausted in February because I had taken things as far as I could on my own and wasn't yielding results. I understand what I was seeking through this Flow Group experience, and I still don't necessarily think that it was bad that I wanted specific things from the weekend. It became a problem when I didn't get those things. I came out of the weekend feeling like a failure and a fool for putting so much pressure on the experience. And so, I just have to forgive myself and be OK with what's going on right now, which is not a whole lot. I look at the goals for the new year and now I need to give myself permission to wipe this board clean and start again.

I get to create a flight to Los Angeles to go to a Michael Beckwith meditation retreat at the end of May. I said "yes" to that thinking that all sorts of financial things were going to happen in Alaska, and they didn't. I feel that familiar nervousness; where's the money going to come from? I feel that shame about, once again, having something to do and seemingly not having money to do it.

It's challenging to vibrationally stay above this sinkhole that always threatens to bring me down. I don't want to feel shame or nervousness. Those feelings are debilitating and don't help me. I'm just hoping that, whatever this all is, it's something meaningful and purposeful. At the same time, I'm reminding myself that there's not something outside of me. I keep looking outside of myself for something to tell me what to do. And even though I may call it God and say I'm seeking God's guidance, in the end I'm the one that has to choose.

Day 43: What Are You Bringing to the Chaos?

I had my weekly affirmative prayer call with Kaleem today, and we started talking about the outer world and what's happening in our country. I believe that the outer world is always a representation of the inner world and that, ultimately, this is really a powerful and important purification time. Not to say that we shouldn't be talking about what's happening or we shouldn't be concerned about what's happening, but that we should be as attentive to what we're each holding internally and individually - whether it's conscious or not, whether it's current or ancestral.

The tough question I ask myself is, "What parts of Donald Trump are in me?" Maybe you might answer: "None." Or maybe there's some compassion and understanding because, at some point, you've been locked in survival mode and wanted to get rid of everything and everyone who threatened you. I think it's important that we balance some of this with this spiritual work that brings us inward. I look at the people surrounding Mr. Trump, and think, *When did I not stand up for truth? When DID I stand up for truth? When did I not do the right thing because I was concerned about what people were going to say? When did I put my needs in front of the collective needs? When did I not take away the keys from the person who shouldn't be driving?*

We have an opportunity to check in first with ourselves and, yes, then certainly hold all these other people accountable to what is going on. Because this is our country. This is our democracy, and this is our government.

If you go to a party or event and the energy feels off, you have a few options. You can walk out. You can become the negative energy of the room. You can also bring your energy to the room. You can be the presence of love and of harmony. You can be the light in the room. That's something I'm working on today. With the time I spend online, looking at the news, I'm thinking: *What I am bringing to a room that's filled with chaos and confusion? What am I doing with my creative powers and my words and my thoughts to help usher in that which I desperately want to see?*

There have to be enough of us who are also willing to turn away from the chaos and drama and turn towards the greater truth seeking to emerge through this specific time. The great Ernest Holmes used to say, "We don't deny the broken leg; it's clearly broken. However, at some point we have to turn away from the leg and the conditions and turn toward a greater truth." If you are spiritually inclined, that means turning from the material world and toward the spiritual world, which comes first.

Truly, we use spiritual laws all the time. When we buy seed packets at the store, we choose based on the end result, what we want to grow. Somehow, packed into the seed, is the fullness of the flower, fruit, or vegetable. I don't know how it works; my job is to pick what I want to grow. I buy seeds knowing the plant is somehow in there. I stick the seed in the cold, dark dirt knowing that it's where it's supposed to go. Somehow everything in the dirt helps the seed crack open. There are these laws that I can't see, the laws of growth, that are going to draw from the seed, through the dense dirt, the thing itself. We can't see this, but that doesn't stop us from expecting to get exactly what we planted. This is happening for us, now. We have to decide: what are we bringing into this room that's clearly filled with chaos and drama?

Donald Trump is who he is. Anybody who thought that Donald Trump was going to show up as a different person in the White House was kidding themselves. Isn't this what people wanted? The very thing he's always been? This is a man who created a reality TV show over firing people and we got off on it as a country. Are we getting off on it now? When we were watching it on reality TV, we weren't necessarily affected by it. It's a different story when the reality TV show is now the President of the United States. It's a different story when your firing of others affects the entirety of a nation. No mistake about it, Mr. Trump is doing the only thing he knows how to do: protect himself and his survival. He's surrounded himself with people who are there to help him with that. So, what is ours to do?

When Barack Obama received the John F. Kennedy award, he said something that stuck with me. He was talking about the wonderful quote from Martin Luther King, Jr. about the long arc of history bending toward justice. He said that the arc doesn't bend on its own. We're here to reach up and grab it with our own lives, acts, and words. We can take hold of that arc and bend it toward that which we desire. That's powerful, and this is a powerful time.

Today I'm realizing that I have to minister to myself. Being confused and uncertain has been a very real experience for me. However today, I'm wondering, is it real or is it a story that I have identified with and consequently, all of my senses tell me that it's real. But what if it isn't? I'm not trying to dismiss my experience, because that doesn't feel right. But I'm sensitive to the stories I tell and my identification as them. As I was praying with and for Kaleem today, I heard a Camille who was tremendously clear, who wasn't confused, and who had a higher perspective. That is all within me for myself, as well. I am my own answer. I have to minister to myself. I have to love and forgive myself and be gentle. I have to reach my hand out to the me that feels like I'm drowning in quicksand and pull. I am powerful.

Day 44: This is What Radical Transformation Requires

I was looking online to learn more about the caterpillar, the chrysalis, and the butterfly. I can relate to many of the magical processes the caterpillar goes through to become the butterfly. I learned that it's incredibly important not to disturb the chrysalis phase; you can kill the caterpillar and the butterfly if you do. This is such a powerful understanding for myself, for you, for all of us. When we are going through the chrysalis - whether you call it the dark night of the soul or depression, the time in which we are deeply in ourselves – we are in the soup of transformation.

It's just an amazingly interesting thing, the soup of transformation. If you could see inside a cocoon, it would seemingly be a gooey mess. But inside the mess are the transformational cells and the newly emerging cells of the butterfly. This meditation experience is like a cocoon, and I call it sacred. I have been going through the transformational stage yet again, and my caterpillar-self knows exactly what to do: die to the old and birth what is seeking to emerge. It's a beautiful and tender way to frame what I'm going through, what we're all going through. It's important to allow for the cocoon and the chrysalis. Know that it's valuable to bow to the need to withdraw or tend to the self; to be quiet and still; to reduce the stimuli of your life. It's purposeful and it's designed to create a space so that a fuller you, a fuller me, can emerge.

I feel the emergence happening today. I'm grateful for that and I allow the process to be and take however long it needs. I'm not rushing anything. I don't want to force myself out of my cocoon faster than the perfect timing of it all. I just trust that, whatever is seeking to come forth, it's emerging from the soup of this transformation.

Transformation is something new coming from the old. Esther Hicks, a powerful speaker and channeler, shows me how to write the new story and how to use my words to design and imagine what I truly want. My words and imagination call things in through the actual story-telling of what I truly desire. Today I realized I don't want to be wrapped up in the world's problems. But I don't want to be completely disconnected from them, either. I want to be right on the edge. I want to be close enough to see and understand the issues and removed enough to be available to the solutions of the problems. If I'm too deep in it, I won't be available to the solutions. I'd be giving up my space to the problem versus being available for the answers seeking to emerge.

This is what I want us to understand. We have an opportunity to be mindful and conscious of what is happening in our country, our state, our community, our family, and in our lives. We have to consciously choose where we're going to stand. I'm consciously choosing to make myself available to ride that edge, to be aware of what's happening, but to also be available to the solution that's seeking to emerge and is coming from the outer world of harmony and peace, a world that works for everyone. I don't want to be a vibrational match to the problem through my words and thoughts. One of the ways that we do that is by speaking the new way. The new way of speaking is not about judging the old way of being in the problem; that's just what's theirs to do, and not mine. It takes a lot of courage and confidence and a sense of clarity to be the one that's not speaking about what's happening, that's not reiterating the story, that's not re-stating the headline. Speaking the new way is to be the one that's coming into the group and saying, "This is what the solution could be. This is what we need to imagine from the chaos and the problem."

There have to be people who are holding the vibrational frequency of the solution within the problem. That's what I want to be. I want to be that for myself, for my family, for my communities, and for this world and this country right now. This is the power we have as individuals. We, the people. This division is really taxing us. Within that is an opportunity to decide what we want to bring to the chaos. Let us choose to release some of our attention from the world of affects, from the headlines, and be the place through which the solution can find some space. I'm grateful for the chrysalis phase and its transformational soup that looks like it's a mess while at the center of it, the butterfly's wings are being formed. The caterpillar chooses to digest itself, to die to itself so that it can create the space for the butterfly to emerge. Wow. Think about this today, deeply, as it relates to your own life. I am.

Day 45: I Got Exactly What I Asked For

After meditation this morning, I watched the video I submitted when I applied for the Flow Group months ago and took some notes about what I'd said.

I'd declared that I was willing to let go of anything and everything getting in the way of me expressing the fullest and greatest Camille that I am here to be. I also talked about the gifts in my life that I'm aware of and how I'm open to the gifts that I haven't yet experienced. What I realized is, that is clarity. Those are also very powerful commands to the Universe and so, clearly, the Universe did the only thing it can do. It said "Yes." When I set my intention for those outcomes, I was probably attached to how that was going to happen. Truthfully, these things have been happening in their own ways. I've been going through a serious transformation. I thought I was done with transformation, as silly as that sounds. In that video I said I'd let go of everything getting in the way of my highest self-expression and make space to experience new gifts and talents – those are really big commands to the Universe.

Now I can see that the meditation fueled the collapse of my internal infrastructure. Over the past 45 days, meditation has allowed me to observe the thoughts of my mind that have mostly been unkind and harsh. These thoughts have set me up to see the world in a way that's not working for me, and all of that has to go to create space for the new me to emerge. This is a big deal. I do have an identity as a radio person. People know that version of me as CC. I have been through my attachment to my own identity, and thought, *If I'm not CC, if I'm not that persona, who and what am I?* We all want the external validation of being seen and heard; we want to know that we matter. I'm recognizing that the collapse my identity, my attachments, my internal thinking structure and the infrastructure of my thoughts must happen for me to have what I say I want: an experience of the greatest Camille Conte I'm here to be.

I'm looking, again, at the whiteboard that had all these core feelings, affirmations, and intentions for how I wanted to shape 2017. I went to erase it, to wipe the slate clean and re-assess what I want to do. When I tried to erase it, there were certain things that didn't come off... how interesting. What remained after I wiped the board? Making an impact. Reach 10,000 people. Emotional frequency that creates my desires. Vibrant strength and health. A steady, growing base income. Regular playfulness. Those aren't bad things to bring into this new day. They make up part of the vision I want to express through my work. Though I'm not sure I experienced all that was advertised for that Flow Group weekend, one thing is certain: I got exactly what I asked for. What a trip! Realizing that this came about differently than I thought it would (or should) also shows me that I had specific expectations pinned to how everything would look. What is it that we really want? Do we really want the things we say we want, or do we want what we want only if it comes into our lives exactly how we think it should? I guess that's the difference between surrender and control.

Today I'm working on being receptive to the Universe. If there's an invisible vortex that is holding the infinite potentiality of my being-ness, wouldn't it just make total sense to receive that instead of pushing to achieve it? We're told we have to make things happen. We have to beat the pavement and be exhausted by the end of the day as proof that we've done it right. But today, I'm going to try something different. I'm going to communicate clearly to the Universe that I am here to receive all the gifts that it has for me.

Day 46: The Heart Knows

It feels like there are changes going on in my heart. I went to see one of my oldest friends last night. We've known each other for 50 years, ever since we were little girls, dreaming big dreams together. She's a remarkable woman and she's incredibly talented and courageous. It was good to see her and to be in the presence of somebody that's known me for so long. We talked about those little-girl dreams, and she said, "I'm living them now. I have peace of mind, I'm not ruled by money, I'm doing the thing I most want to do, which is paint, and I know things are going to turn." We talked about Colonel Sanders and all these people that hit their stride later in their lives. We talked about how our lives look nothing like the lives most of us were prepared to live, growing up.

Her declarations and our conversation inspired me and tuned me in to the sense of change inside my heart. It feels a little scary, but I'm just observing it. I guess it feels scary because it has to do with where I live, in and in-between Alaska and New Jersey, and what I want. I realize that I'm desiring a great love in my life and wondering where I need to be for that experience to manifest. I'm thinking about my mom and the future and all that I want to come to pass. Things are being rearranged in my heart, and I'm actually able to bear witness to the process and possible outcomes. I wonder if the caterpillar has this awareness when it begins to rearrange its own organs to become the butterfly? If not, that could be a hugely distressing time. I'm thankful for my awareness of my heart.

Day 47: A Mother and Child Reunion

Today is Mother's Day, and I have a really great mom. She appropriately makes me crazy. She's very hip and is a wonderful supporter of my dreams and my confusion. We had a lovely time together. My mom used to work in a salon as a manicurist, and she's still quite good at it. I have my father's fingers and never really went for nail color or anything, but my mom wanted to do manicures. We were sitting together and as she was filing my nails, she asked me a question: "Why exactly are you going back to Alaska?" It was an interesting moment, one where I didn't necessarily have an answer. I thought, *What is going on?* I was talking about the projects I've been involved in and some of the seemingly un-manifested intentions and being uncertain about where to go.

She said, "I never had that. When I was growing up I never had the opportunity to ask those questions. I never had the kind of life where I was thinking about what I wanted to do and then how I was going to do it." In her generation, women grew up with a very specific roadmap: get married, have children, be a wife and a mother. It was a beautiful, eye-opening moment to sit there with my mom, who is 86, going on about my stuff and my perceived problems only to hear her express envy that she didn't have the chance to think the way I was thinking. She didn't have the chance to dream the way I'm able to dream. It just really touched my heart.

Today, I'm going to put all of my self-centered analysis down after this video. Today I'm going to be fully available and fully in love with my mom. I'm going to laugh with her and take pictures and celebrate all that she's sacrificed to be a mother of three daughters. I'm grateful that she's alive. I'm looking forward to spending the day with my mom and my sister Janice, all of us missing my other sister in Alaska. I give thanks for these powerful, strong women who have shown me what it's like to be a mom. They are all tremendous inspirations to me, and they also inspire me to be mindful of the mothering we do for ourselves.

So to the mother within me that mothers the child within me, I say, "Happy Mother's Day." It is indeed a mother and child reunion, on many levels.

Day 48: The Grand Design of Me is Activated

Today has been a very powerful morning. I'm appreciative of

what is happening in me and what is emerging from me. I just came out of my meditation and had a powerful affirmative prayer.

One of the great benefits of being back in New Jersey with my family is being able to so clearly see the patterns I've absorbed along the way that no longer serve me. One of the biggest default patterns that I have within me are the expectations about people or things outside of me satisfying a need within me. That always, always leads to disappointment. It's an illusion of control, and it's a misunderstanding of who and what is my source. People outside of me – my family, my friends, society – are not my source. But we've been told that they are, and I was walking around subtly and subconsciously needing people to say certain things or do certain things or act in ways that I thought I needed them to act.

I don't want that anymore. I don't want anyone outside of myself to be responsible for what is mine to source and do. And the truth of the matter is that my source, this invisible essence of Love Intelligence, is already within me. This is the inward journey. When we moved into 2017, I was super clear. I wanted to be influential in this life. I wanted to help 10,000 people take the inward journey and set their real selves free. I didn't know it at the time, but with that expressed desire came the humbling understanding and clarity that I have to do this myself first, and as I do it, I'm uncovering so many stories and expectations.

This is another thing that's really blowing my mind today. There's a difference between the momentum of the heart and the momentum of the past. The momentum of the past is what I've been observing by having these hour-long meditations. Why does my mind want to recreate the past? Because the mind is most comfortable with what's known and expected. When the heart says, "Let's do this new thing," it's coming from that field of infinite possibilities and so the mind comes rushing in and squashes it.

That inspiration to try something new contains a seed, and within it is everything that's necessary for the new growth and expression. But the mind comes in and tries to convince us that the heart doesn't know; how could it know? It's coming from nothing! The mind is coming at least from something that it knows. It works its way into the psyche, and the next thing you know you've crushed your heart's desire and you don't do the thing you want to do.

I'm thinking about going back to Alaska and working where I worked last summer. I called them last week – wonderful people, great conversation – but they told me that they were already staffed. The first experience I had was this feeling of constriction and doors closing on me. And I realized – wait a minute – that's my mind thinking that what I did last year, I have to do this year. That is your mind collapsing an infinite field of fresh and new possibilities for this summer into what it knew last year. The truth of the matter is, maybe my highest good isn't at that job. Maybe it's not about forcing this year to look like last year.

I'm in a completely different space. I said I wanted to live from my heart; maybe this summer something is trying to emerge that doesn't look like last year. Instead of feeling bad or finding more evidence that something is working against me or finding more evidence that makes me depressed, I'm saying hold on a second! That's my mind talking. What is my heart saying today?

This Michael Beckwith retreat and how it came to be is so powerful for me. I said yes to this meditation retreat back in February, before I even submitted my application to go to the Flow Group and before I knew I'd be meditating for 100 days! But I needed something to resuscitate myself, so the first thing I set in motion was this meditation retreat. I stepped into the reality of that yes and reserved my place, knowing I would go but not fully knowing how it would work out. And now, several months later, it's coming up and I've been delaying getting my airline ticket. Now, I'm looking at tickets and thinking, *So you didn't buy an airline ticket when it was $200 because your mind told* *you that you had to know all these things first*. Had I just bought the ticket months ago, I would've known all of those things. I could have created certainty out of uncertainty with that purchase. Now, of course, the tickets are much more expensive. There's my lack and limitation mind telling me that I have no income and all of this stuff. But you know what? I have a credit card. Though it's not ideal to have debt on a credit card, I do have one. Even more than that, I have an awareness today that the same Intelligence that allowed me to hear about and be selected to go to the retreat with Kyle also put together the unbelievably specific details that allowed me to be financially able to go. That's the same intelligence that's working through this meditation weekend with Michael Beckwith, and it's worlds beyond my finite thinking.

The trip of it is, when I came out of that retreat with Kyle, what did I commit to? More meditation than I've ever done in my life. I've been meditating for 48 days now, and next weekend I'm going to be sitting in meditation with Michael Beckwith, and 100 other people for an entire weekend. I've literally been training for this, but I had no idea this is how things would shake out. That is the infinite field of potentiality communicating to me that this is mine. The idea to commit to reconnecting with myself unfolded beyond what I could have ever imagined. Esther Hicks says that, by the time an idea comes to us, it is already 99% complete. That's why it arrives as an inspired idea.

But what do we do with inspired ideas? Often we say, "How am I going to make this happen?" I do, anyway. And with that, we immediately stunt the arrival of that which is already mostly done. Pinning down the How is not mine to do. As creators, that's not ours to do. Within the inspired idea is potential momentum, the Law of Attraction, the substance of Life itself. What's mine to do is to say, "Let's go!" To welcome the idea, to allow it. But that's such a completely revolutionary way of thinking. We've been told that, when you get an inspiration, you gotta go make it happen. That's not what this is about. This is understanding that it already has happened. That it's already arriving. Saying yes is the first step.

It's just like the seed. How the hell is it possible for the full expression of a rose to be in a tiny seed? We know that it is. We trust that it is. We believe that it is. We expect that seed to produce the thing we want. I am accepting that Infinite Intelligence now has room to emerge through me as the perfect purchase of my airline ticket. And wherever I go after that, whether back to New Jersey or Alaska, I'm fired up.

Day 49: Daughters Caring for Mothers

It's many hours after meditation. Today I'm feeling the shame I usually feel when I lose my cool with my mom. Being a caregiver and being a daughter caring for her mom while living together is every single thing. It's joy, sadness, fun, grief, ease and flow, and tremendous frustration. It calls on me to go to a depth of my compassion and my unconditional love and a way of being in service that is truly beyond anything I've ever done before.

Fortunately, my mom and I have the kind of relationship where I can always go back and apologize to her, and we always come back to love. I'm grateful for that, because the pressure was on. I was searching online to get that airline ticket to Los Angeles and found a ticket at a great price: one seat left. I went to get it, went to get it, went to get it, but it wasn't going through. It turns out it wasn't really an available seat and the price had actually gone up while trying to buy it. I was finally able to get the ticket using every credit card I have, only to feel the shame of having no more available credit there.

I was feeling frustrated that yesterday was such a powerful day of ease and flow and today was like – wow, what happened? I went for a walk and calmed down and spoke to the God of my understanding and asked for a sign that It was hearing me and helping me reconcile these seeming opposites. On instinct, I turned around and went through the park, on a path that leads through the little forest into the open field. All of a sudden, from the side, here comes a butterfly. I have to say, that's a sign I can understand, in a language I can understand.

I have a ticket to Los Angeles, and that's all I have. That's all I know today.

Day 50: How Can I Live Fully from My Heart Without the Dismantling of My Mind?

WOW. I'm at the halfway point in my experiment. 50 days! What are some of the things that I know after 50 days of doing this? I know that there is still an aspect of my mind that resists going into that meditation every single morning, that says, "I don't want to do this. We don't have to do this. Let's not do this."

I also know that there are times when 60 minutes goes by in a flash. There are other times we it feels like the most painful, 4-hour-long 60 minutes that could ever exist in time and space. I know that I am more distant from my thoughts. I've become more of an observer of my thoughts. That has been an avenue to insight and inspiration. Being in observer's mode and being able to watch from a high perch has allowed me to see all sorts of patterns of thinking that have really been detrimental to my growth and health and peace of mind. I can see that they've kept me stuck, small, and "safe" in what's familiar and have gotten in the way of living fully from my heart.

What could be more important to the goal of living from my heart than the dismantling of my mind? One is certainly leading to the other. I know that I'm living on the edge of my own life. I'm going to this retreat with Michael Beckwith, and I don't have any information about where to go after that or how I'm going to pay to go wherever I'm inspired to go after that. It's absolutely incredible. I feel pretty light and OK with it, because it's so outrageous and funny that I'm just like, OK sure! When you ain't got nothing, you got nothing to lose.

I can't lose all that I have, the most important thing of which is my consciousness and heart. All of the things I hold most valuable, I can't lose them. They're inherently mine, part of the eternal. I'm feeling good, and that's a good thing. I hope you are, too. If you're not, remember: tell the story that makes you feel good. Even if you can't see the evidence of it, tell the story anyway until you start feeling as good as if it's actually there. And sure enough, it's on its way.

Day 51: Emotional Rescue

Today is an emotional day for me; I have these days when I come to New Jersey. First of all, it's 90-something degrees and I'm way out of my comfort zone. I have to have the air conditioner on because, otherwise, it's not a good scene. Also, when I'm here I don't maintain a healthy balance between serving myself and serving my mom. This is a challenge because I'm in the house she's in. I don't have another place to retreat, just have this room upstairs. And though I'm grateful for it, it's difficult to balance putting the oxygen mask on myself and being of service to my mom. Next week I'm leaving for L.A. and I don't think I'm coming back for the summer. The best I can do is what I always do, which is to set my mom up with all sorts of good food, make a lot of meals and freeze them, and pull the Jersey family members in. That's the best I can do as I try to lay a foundation for my own life.

There's a lot of stuff going on in all of our personal lives, our families, our extended communities, our country, and in the world. Within all that, I have to stay committed to my emotional, vibrational journey and to feeling joy and peace at all costs. I have to do my spiritual practices that keep me centered in my real self that is eternal, not touched by the world of affects and the craziness going on around us. I don't know any other answer but to turn within, to turn toward my practices of meditation, prayer, quiet contemplation, walking, and healthy eating. I don't know much more than that. So that's where I'm going to keep my attention today.

Day 52: I'm Sitting with the One that Knows. Listen Deeply

I had a deep meditation today. At one point I heard this voice that I always hear: *Why are we doing this? It's taking too long. Look at the clock, this is enough. It's Saturday. We have so much to do.* Then I heard another voice that said, "Stay in the seat." I realized OK, don't get attached to those thoughts that are telling me to look at the clock. I've done that before. Just let it be. At some point toward the end of my meditation, I heard, "You're sitting with the One that Knows. Listen deeply."

I settled in more deeply, whatever that means or however that happened. I thought, Wow. I'm sitting with the One that Knows. I need to remember that It is inside me. It is in this gap, this space that I create in meditation, between the silence and the stimuli; between the inner world and the outer world. You, too, are sitting with the One That Knows. Listen deeply. On my end, I'm choosing to allow that to settle within me in a deep and profound way. I am the One, and I am with the One that knows. The only thing to do is to listen deeply. I'm really spending these days talking to my heart, asking it to speak to me, and then listening intently.

Day 53: Honesty is a Choice

Honesty is a choice. To be real and authentic is absolutely a choice. There are many times when I come to this video with something in me that doesn't want to be honest. I know that's my ego, because my ego wants me to present this perfect experience to you. My ego wants to present an outcome: a specific, positive, measurable, productive outcome from 53 days of meditation. My ego doesn't want me to be confused or uncertain; it doesn't want to own up to feeling the way I feel. It's a choice, today, to turn on this camera and be real.

I'm going to see some high school friends I grew up with. I'm already thinking about how honest I'll be about how I feel. If you go to someone whose well is empty and you're looking for support or an understanding ear, you don't always get the compassion you may have thought you were going to get. It can be very uncomfortable when you're open, raw, and the person you're talking to is not able to deal with that. In that case, my heart closes. I retreat inward, putting up my protective walls and saying, "Nope! Never again. I'm not doing this." It's a constant choice to open the heart over and over when all it wants to do, often, is close as a form of protection. Close off from the stimuli, the feeling state, the craziness happening in our world. It takes mindful intention and action to stay open in the midst of all of this.

This is one of the more challenging times of my life. It hasn't been this uncertain in a long, long time. I still feel unsettled and indecisive. Man alive, those are uncomfortable feelings. Is it uncomfortable because I'm resisting it? Maybe. All I can do is say, "I feel uncomfortable and I love that." I feel indecisive, and I embrace that. I feel confused and unsure, and I'm loving that too." That's the idea, to unclench the fists of resistance by acknowledging the issue and loving it so it can dissolve and the heart stays open. We keep the heart open.

My ego is definitely active today. It's already telling me to shut this down, I've said too much. And all I can do is love that, too. That egoic voice of survival, it comes out of fear and needs approval and love. It does all things to be seen and loved.

But I've seen some anger come out of myself these last few days, and I guess I have to love that too. I've seen myself be very agitated and annoyed and say mean-spirited things. All I can do is keep coming back to the forgiveness, and my heart, and to just stay with whatever is happening. Right now, it feels like I should have a different story after going 53 days into this experiment. I'm going to sit with gratitude and raise my vibration a little bit and prepare myself to go to Asbury Park to meet up with some girlfriends. I'm looking forward to an afternoon of laughter and accepting each other exactly as we are. It will be wonderful.

Day 54: Life is What Happens to You When You're Making Other Plans

Thirty-seven minutes into my meditation this morning, my mom called me from the bottom of the stairs. She couldn't get her earring in her ear as she's getting ready to go to bingo. She was clearly frustrated. I choose to come out of my meditation and go downstairs to help her. I helped her finish dressing and made sure she had everything she needed. After she left, I finished the hour of silence.

Yesterday, I drove to Asbury Park to meet up with some friends; three of us, girlfriends all the way back to grammar school and high school. It was a wonderful thing to come together as grown women and laugh and remember and dream, to dare ourselves to keep our hearts open.

An open heart is a choice, just like honesty. I've been watching these videos that we received after going through the Flow Group weekend, and the one I'm on now is talking all about the heart, closed as well as open. It was talking about how the closed heart often comes from our own inner resistance that we build up whether we're aware of it or not. A closed heart is also a result of being in an argument with ourselves, being against ourselves. The video also talked about how you have to become OK with all of that in order to keep the heart open.

That was exactly what I was saying earlier with my friends as we were walking on the boardwalk yesterday. How, in the face of pain and uncertainty, keeping the heart open is a courageous act. And yet, that's where it all is. The open heart knows that there's more to existence, and yet it doesn't know all the details. It's not necessarily supposed to know the How of the details. Yet, nestled inside of it is the How. But you've got to be in the open heart before you can get all those juicy details. Why would all of the details of the How be released to something that's not fully committed and ready?

Today is a very frizzy-haired Monday, and I strongly experienced the urge to close my heart earlier today, after getting in an argument with another person. I made the choice not to close, and I'm now standing in the midst of an open heart, very much like these gorgeous flowers outside of my mom's window that have been tightly closed buds. But something deep within them is causing them to bloom and stretch the green skin that encased them, pushing that back as the petals begin to appear and open, seemingly without pain. But you know that, somewhere inside there, something uncomfortable is happening. As Anais Nin said, "The time came when it was more painful to remain in the closed, tight bud than what it took to bloom." The open heart is the bloom.

Day 55: I am a Perfect Expression of a Perfect Love

Visiting my girlfriends has stirred up a lot in me, particularly the conversation we had about the book, "Illusions," by Richard Bach. When we were 18, my friends and I read that book, a book that laid the foundation of an attitude that's been with us, with me all this time, and has forever shaped my life. We started talking about our age and how youthful we feel and look, and how people are often like, "What? You can't be that age!" One of my friends said, "It's our attitude." And it's true. That book and the beliefs we cultivated at such an early age made us choose to believe that anything is possible, that limitations and walls are all illusions.

And now Richard Bach is releasing "Illusions 2: Tales of a Reluctant Student." My friend gave each of us this book on Sunday as we sat on the beach, on the old lifeguard chair, just like we'd done so many years ago. We stared out at the ocean with few words and full hearts, our minds swimming in and out of past, present, and future time.

Who would have ever thought there would be an "Illusions 2?" Richard Bach never thought it would happen, but here it is. The thread that runs through this book is the illusions of death, injury, and permanent damage while exploring the power of affirmations to communicate, from the spirit to our minds and bodies, a truth we believe in but cannot see. This is really the crux of the teaching that I brought into this year, 2017. Taking the inward journey. Turning away from effects. Turning inward. Connecting with my real self and setting that free. I marvel at the perfection of it all. I marvel at my mind's focus on the imperfection of it all. I'm grateful for the meditation that has distanced me from the two so that I can simply see with the eyes of Spirit what is true.

In a couple of days I will grab a small suitcase and fly to L.A. to meditate with Dr. Michael Beckwith and 99 other people who are going off to the desert to be in silence for at least 48 hours. I'll carpool out with a wonderful woman I connected with. I'm affirming that someone will house me for a few days after the retreat. I feel like I need to be someplace where no one knows me so I can decompress and gather myself with no demands from the outside world. No caretaking roles; no roles at all.

Day 56: I Surrender

Today my video-avoidant self had to record not just one, but two videos after I accidentally deleted the first one. That's just kind of how the day's been going. I'm trying to print out my boarding pass but that's not working either. I'm feeling the need to surrender, and that's what I'm going to do. I'm going to let this all be. But because I have this commitment to do these videos, I had to throw something on even though it's 10:30 at night.

Today, I had an unfortunate moment in which I chose to be an expression less than love. Like a riptide, I got caught in the undercurrent of a high drama exchange and ended up yelling and participating in a shouting match, after which I felt very sad and heavy and shameful that I didn't opt for a higher choice. Then I realized what was mine to do was to apologize, and my ego was immediately like, "We're not apologizing! They did this, and we were right, and they were wrong." On and on. I realized that, if I'm going to be the vibration of love, I have to at least get back to the vibration of love as soon as I realize I've left it.

So, I called and left a sincere apology. I have to figure this out. I have to figure out how to remain calm and tethered to my source, connected to the truth of who I am, without getting charged up and triggered and reacting from a place less than love. I've got plenty of opportunities to master this – plenty! I had several just today, but I didn't choose to master that in the moment.

I'm going to keep trying. I'm going to keep thanking everybody who's coming into my life and doing whatever they're doing to help me master this, because I really want to. I really want to be the vibration of love. How am I ever going to get onto the higher vision of why I am alive in this particular time if I can't master interpersonal relationships? When I say master, I get that I'm human and will slip up. But I'm disappointed that, today, I went unconscious, or – worst of all – I stayed unconscious, and kept going. I'm disappointed I didn't pull one of the hundreds of different ways I could have dealt with the situation from my tool bag. But you know what? It's over now, many hours ago. So why am I keeping it alive with my word?

Tomorrow morning I'm off to California. When I told my soul brother, Kaleem, about only having a one-way ticket, he said, "That's it, there's no coming back!" In other words, there's no turning back now. And sure, I'm eventually coming back to this place, but there's something outrageous and perfect about the metaphor. I have a couple hundred dollars in my bank account and no ticket to come back, and yet I feel at peace and totally supported because something higher is at work here. Maybe it's my own insanity – we'll see. But whatever it is, I'm living from my heart right here and right now. Free falling.

****

I'm stepping out of the flow of my videos to talk about Michael Beckwith and to set up my weekend meditation retreat that

I wrote about in the beginning of the book.

Remember how I didn't have the pull anymore to go to Hawaii but instead got inspired to go to the meditation retreat? At the time, I just thought it was a singular event with no connection to anything else that was happening, but I don't believe that anymore. Now I believe that this was one of the imaginal discs in my transformation. These synchronistic events were already planned out by my soul long before I was able to connect the dots. I now know that this is why the desire fell away from going to Maui. I was supposed to go to the meditation retreat. It was part of the divine order of my life permanently changing. Think about it: I signed up for a meditation weekend, something I'd never done, before I knew that I'd be committing to meditating an hour every day for 100 days, something I'd also never done. So back in February, when Michael Beckwith and Kyle Cease were dominating my life in the same week and I didn't think twice about it, the Power that breathes me already knew there was more to come.

And that's not all. While I was in the Flow Group, Kyle's book, "I Hope I Screw this Up" was heading to the New York Times Bestseller list. He was so excited and was sharing the news with us as texts were coming in from his agent. Then he casually mentioned who wrote the foreword to his book. Any guess? Yep. His good friend, Michael Beckwith.

All of this was dancing in my mind as I flew to L.A. for the meditation retreat. I decided not to run any videos during the retreat in order to honor the silence and eliminate my interaction with all technology. I wanted to be fully available for whatever might happen. Also the morning after the retreat ended, I was feverish and without a voice. This healing crisis lasted several days upon my return to New Jersey, so a total of nine days went by without me rolling tape. What follows is the nine-day video summary I did of what happened during that time.

****

57: Upping My Game

I flew to L.A. on Thursday morning and joined 100 other people for a meditation retreat. As Michael Beckwith says, we retreat to advance. It was an amazing experience at Royal Ranch Way, 900 sacred acres of land out in the Lucerne Valley. You've had that experience, right, where you are literally feeling the vibration of the earth under your feet and through you? That was my experience at Royal Ranch. It took 30 years for these people to shape the ranch into the gorgeous place it is today, and it was just a blessing. Lisa Solis Delong, the woman who picked me up and drove me to the retreat, was also a blessing. Each person who crossed my path was absolutely placed there purposefully, and I'm so grateful for it all.

Lisa is also in her 50s and is a dancer, an author, and a nurse. She's written a book titled "Blood Brothers." She's been on the speaking circuit with her book and is now also asking the question, "What else is seeking to emerge?"

After arriving at the ranch, we immediately went to check in and find out which house we're assigned to, some of which are a fair distance from the main building. They showed us the map, and my housing for the weekend was extremely far from the main area. So immediately my mind was telling me, *This is a bad thing! How dare they put me so far away from everything! I registered way back in February; shouldn't that mean something now?* Immediately, my mind was presenting this housing as a less-than situation for me - that because of where I was assigned to stay, I was going to have a less-than experience. I was listening to my mind present this to me, and finally I interrupted it and said, "That can't be true because this is where I'm being put. There must be a reason why I'm there."

Lisa drove me to the house because it was about a 15 or 20-minute walk from the main area. I walk into a huge room with 8 single beds lined up, however the woman there assigning beds said to me, "You're in the back room. It has it's own bath as well." And who was my roommate, but Jen Carlson! Who is Jen

Carlson? She's a punk rock drummer who was just working the Desert Trip Concert with Neil Young, Bob Dylan, and Paul McCartney! My rock 'n roll, radio-show-producing heart was ecstatic. So, was I in the right place? Absolutely. Jen and I had an amazing experience and, before the weekend was over, we were already talking about when we'd get to connect again. She's a wonderful woman and getting to know her was an amazing experience.

Day 58: Learn to be Still

I learned a lot about meditation from Michael Beckwith, who is a powerful teacher. To be in such an intimate setting, learning with and from him and 100 other people – that changed my life.

I've never done that much meditation at once. Michael said something so profound and simple about meditation, that meditation is the practice of honing the skill to be still, of being able to observe your thoughts. I'd never heard it put like that before. It was all about placing our intention and then being mindful of our attention. We came into this new understanding about meditation being something that strengthens our muscles and our ability to be still and observe. We disentangle ourselves from our thoughts. We no longer identify ourselves as our thoughts, and we can see that there's a Mind behind the mind. We're able to step out of the mind that's in front of the Mind: the only Mind that really is. We're able to take that seat and observe. It was just so powerful.

Day 59: Practicing this Art of Being Still

We started our first meditation at 6:00 am. I proved to myself that I could get up at 5:00 am if I wanted to, and I really wanted to. And what a committed group this was! A couple flew in from China. Three people, including myself, flew in from New Jersey. The power in the room was really great because everybody was there to up their game and go deeper.

Day 60: I'm Ready for Change

After the retreat, I left the ranch with a new friend, Deb. And what does Deb do for a living? She runs a housing property for seniors. I'm a daughter living with her mother at this time, and I'm involved in a senior community, in reality. So there's Deb, who is not only a property manager, but also the social activity coordinator. No accidents there! I got a chance to see what it looks like for another woman in her 50s to put all of her love into helping seniors have a beautiful living environment. It was really touching.

Deb and I drove from her house to Agape International, where Michael Beckwith is the spiritual leader. We got up at 5:00 am and had to be on the road at 5:30 to be at the 6:30 service. All of the meditators from the retreat were there, as well as a handful of other people. We stayed on for the 9:30 service and I swear, it was like being at a Baptist revival. I've never actually been to one, but I've heard about them, maybe seen them on TV. I caught the fire! I don't know at what point that I stood up, but I was on my feet as this beautiful song was being sung – "I surrender, Everything that I've been holding onto I let go.....I'm ready for my change." Yes I am.

Day 61 and Day 62: Letting Go of My Storyline

I had no idea I had so many stories, but I did. I went through a healing crisis after the meditation retreat. So much had been dislodged in my system and was seeking a way out. Everybody wanted to say I had a cold, but I knew it wasn't. I knew what came up during that weekend: the patterns of thinking that have a coagulated energy around them. I got to see them from that far distance that meditation offers and I got to let them go when I saw all the stories that have made my life more difficult than it ever needs to be, all the identities I'm still clinging to.

I'll share with you one more profound realization I had. While I love music and I love rock 'n roll, what I heard was: *it's too limiting*. The expression of me as a rock 'n roll DJ is too limiting. I need to open that up wider. I've been feeling that, but to really see that as an identity that needs to fall away or expand was really incredible. That's the core identity I've been holding on to. This is who I am. This is what I do. Over the weekend I thought, *Are you ready to let go of that?* The answer is, I am. I can feel something more powerful seeking to emerge. I don't know exactly what it is, but I know it's seeking space. I'm releasing stories. I'm releasing my identity.

Day 63: Back in New Jersey

And just like that, I'm back in New Jersey. After the healing crisis, I was down for the count. I have no voice, but inside I'm still processing quite a bit and still having a lot of emotional release. What a privilege and gift it is that I'm spending my life this way, that this is my life. I'm not getting up and going to a job from 8-5. I have this incredibly unique gift that is my life. I get to spend my adult days exactly like this, attending to my soul.

Day 64: Clearing the Stories that Limit Me

Yesterday I got to see another story and identity that my sister pointed out to me: managing the emotional container of my family. I grew up as the youngest of the family, amidst a lot of drama – as I'm sure there was for your family. I grew up during the 70s, during the Vietnam War and the Women's Movement. There was a lot of change and pressure in the family and a lot of roles that were going through significant transition.

I became the emotional manager of my family. I still do this. In my meditation yesterday, I asked to be shown any lingering stories that I'm not aware of. I want to clear these and be available to be the revealer of love and the divine light that is nestled at the center of each of our beings.

Day 65: "Tell everyone on the train that I love them."

I came out of the meditation weekend, dabbled in the headlines and saw the news about the two men who stood against a racist and were killed on a train in Portland. That has deeply moved me. The thing about the heart is, there are these moments where you feel like it can't open any wider. You think it can't open anymore, but it can. It can always open a little more. When I read the story of those two heroes on the train, a 23-year-old man and a 53-year-old man, both filled with that divine impulse to protect and care for others, my heart broke wide open. When I read the mother's first response after losing her son – "In spite of this, we choose love." – my heart opened even wider. We choose love. It's a choice.

Then I read about the woman who took off her shirt and put it under the 23-year-old's head and held his hand. All she knew to do was to pray with him. She told him how wonderful he was, and he looked at her and said, "Tell them, tell everyone on the train, that I love them." At that point my heart just burst into a million, gazillion pieces of the stardust that it's made up of.

That, my friend, is everything. This life is the train. That is everything this 23-year-young soul was here to teach. It was a powerful lesson. When he said, "tell everyone. . . ", that included the racist man with the knife who murdered him. That's the ability to see beyond the veil of separation. That's the ability to see beyond the appearance of love and hate. That is all that we need to know to change this world. Tell everyone on the train that I love them.

Maybe the train is your relationship, family, work environment, community, friendship circle, country, the world – whatever train you're on right now, join me in choosing to be the vibration of love, no matter the appearance. This is the time to set your real self free. This is the time to embrace meditation. Sit down, even if it's for 60 seconds, and begin to practice being still. There is a You behind the you that you know. It has every-thing you could ever want or need. We are tethered to an unbounded, inexhaustible source.

I'm leaping. I have no idea what that means, but I know what it feels like – exhilarating and scary at the same time. It feels like this chrysalis phase is over and it's time for me to spread my wings and leap. What would it be like if we all just allowed our hearts to open?

Join me, today, in choosing love.

Day 66: I am Letting Go of a 53-Year-Old Story and Identity

The side effect of meditating this long, this consistently, is that I have developed the skill to observe and untangle myself from my thoughts. I have come to realize that I am not my thoughts. I have been able to realize that my identity, my sense of self, is not my thoughts. It's pretty big. I've created a lot of space and, as a result of that, things are coming up through that open-ness. Yesterday, I shared two things that are remaining to be very powerful revelations, big boulders dislodged from my psyche. I have been observing them like a doctor with a patient on the operating table. One is, the little-girl Camille has got my attention.

I've been doing a practice for myself that I also do with my clients, to find the younger versions of ourselves and bring them home. I realized that I had to go get that little Camille and bring her home to my heart today. She came out in a very big way when it was brought to my attention that I took on the role of family peacekeeper at an early age. I did this to control the emotional context in my family. I used my humor to deflect and to shift people's attention. I used my tears to cause an interrup-tion to the fighting. There was a lot of fighting and arguing. As the youngest one, it touched me deeply and I didn't like it. I didn't want it. I still don't.

Having this realization and having this little Camille come out and talk to me about the heaviness that she's been carrying all this time has been humbling. In sessions with my clients, I can hear the little girl or little boy in their story, and I take them back to get that child. I have them sit with that little person and simply listen to what their younger self has to say. Then I have them pick that little person up and carry them back to the heart. I've done that for myself today because I have continued to maintain that young-child role of emotional manager. I don't want it anymore. I can't even begin to tell you the weight that is being lifted from me. This experience that's happening today, these emotional releases that I am having as a result of this realization along with the release of my 53-years long identity of peacekeeper at my own expense, is unique. It's completely different to choose to be the vibration of peace than to work to keep and contrive peace. This is huge, and is giving me such emotional release. I am grateful that I have this day, here and now, to be present for my transformation and healing. I'm so grateful that this is my life. There's got to be a reason why this is my full-time job.

The other big piece that continues to work its way loose within me is this identity around my radio work. My willingness to continue looking at this story has caused it to be amplified in my awareness. This goes all the way back to 2013 when I traveled away from Alaska. Even before that, I was beginning to feel this spiritual Camille that I wanted to integrate into my work. How could I integrate these Camilles together, the radio DJ, CC, and this spiritual Camille? I've wanted to integrate all of myself unto myself for quite some time. My DJ identity has been sacred to me. I have clung to it and I have fought for it. Part of me is thinking, *I gotta bring this forward, but I don't want to let go. This is who I am, I'm not giving this up.*

The thing is, it's not about giving it up. It's not necessarily about the identity as much as it's about my attachment to the identity. Rather, it's about my attachment to seeing myself as being limited to this particular expression. And so, once the genie's out of the bottle, you can't stuff it back in. This revelation, awareness, and the willingness to move through it all is exactly what I said I wanted. This is living from the heart. This is being willing to make space in my old identities and expressions for something new to grow and expand.

I just can't encourage you enough to be in your practices, whatever they are, that unhook you from the world of affects. Whatever it is that removes you from the headlines or takes you out of the conversations where people are just regurgitating the news. Remove yourself. Take a break. Go for a walk. Get your feet on Mother Earth. Get out into the woods, the beach, take a hike, do something for your soul. Begin to ask, "What is it within that's seeking to emerge?" Have the courage and the willingness to be mindful of any stories that don't serve you anymore or identities that you're clinging to out of fear. It's courageous work but today I can't imagine any other work worth doing.

Day 67 - I'm Turning in My Victim Card

Something happened for me in my meditation practice today. I was made so clearly aware of the subtle remaining victim stories. I've always prided myself on having cleared out my victim consciousness, and to a great extent, I have. However, with a new definition and a new understanding of what the ego is, I have been seeing more into my own ego than ever before. I am seeing the ways in which my ego has kept me at a distance, almost at war, with myself. Fighting against myself, fighting against my own identities and various personalities. I have these lingering victim stories, these threads, that I saw today in a way that was very powerful and very healing. Right now, I am in a situation that can feed the victim story. I have chosen things that, if I'm unaware, can be misused to weave the "poor me, why is this always happening to me" story.

I'm waking up to that, and I'm handing in my victim card. I'm giving it back, because victimhood is yet another way that I stay tethered to the world outside of myself. Victimhood fools me into believing that things or people outside of me are the source of my luck, love, approval – on and on that list goes. I'm giving back my victim card today and taking full responsibility for every single activity, action, and thought of my life. I'm taking full responsibility and full accountability AND I am remembering the truth: my life is a fully-sourced gift.

I was watching a presentation that Michael Beckwith gave online, and he said that all has been given to us already and our practices help us receive it. This is about the receptive mode. My situation here in New Jersey is such that I am not working a typical full-time job. I'm not even working a part-time job. The job I'm really working is being in service to my mother. This is something I'm choosing to do now. I've been away from New Jersey for 25 years and my mom is 86, and I'm choosing this situation. It's been a bit of a balancing act to make this work and figure out how I'm going to pay my bills.

This is an opportunity for me to go even deeper and to realize that, if I'm fully sourced and all of my needs are met in the spiritual world, the only thing I have to do is to speak the story of it already being in my life. As Esther Hicks says, in my vibrational vortex everything is 99.9% complete. I just have to speak it. I really do have a full-time job, and I'm excited about how the Universe is going to bring this into my experience, because now I know what my part is. My part is to look beyond the appearance that says things are not being manifested in my life. My job is to look beyond the numbers in my bank account that are trying to tell me a story about my identity that is not the truth of who I am. My job is to be really clear about what it is I want to experience, what lights me up, and what expands me. My job is to be clear about the leaps I am taking, right now, today, to get this message, my teaching and me out into the world. And then my job is to simply move and be in the vibrational alignment of what that is.

I am open. I am open to all of the many ways that financial good is coming into my life. I'm open to serving seniors, I'm open to raking lawns, and I'm also open to sitting in the silence long enough to feel, in-my-bones-deep, the spiritual truth that all my needs are met. That's what I think is so cool about Jesus - and whether you think he's the real thing or a character in a story, it doesn't matter. What's so interesting about Jesus is that he was so lined up with his Source that he didn't need a purse. He didn't need things because he truly felt, in his bones, his oneness with All That Is. He was in alignment with all that had already been given to him. Anytime he needed something, it was just there because his consciousness was already there. I'm fascinated with that. To a great extent, I've designed my life to prove that.

My hope for you is that you realize your feelings are the most powerful part of the creation process, because feelings are the creative juice of that which is manifested. And if 99.9% of all your good is already done, what story are you telling? Are you telling the story of that which is already done, even though you can't see it? Are you playing that game? Or are you playing the other game, where you're looking into the world of affects and telling that story of lack, limitation, and not-enoughness? What is your vibrational address?

Day 68: There Is Hope

Today I want to talk about hope. My friend's son is mourning the loss of a friend that took his life through suicide. We were just talking about how a lot of people feel hopeless right now. And guess what? There are just as many people that feel very hope-FULL. What's the difference? The biggest piece I can see is the inward journey. We are waking up – sometimes painfully – to a very important awareness and understanding. The template we've been resting our lives on, the formula we've been told to use to have a successful and fulfilling life, turns out to be outdated. The crux of that formula has us resting all of our hope on the thing I call the world of affects. The external world. The material world.

We're seeing the material world collapse under the weight of its own outdated matrix. Something new is seeking to emerge, a balanced understanding that – before the material – there is the spiritual. Before the plant, there is the seed. We are witnessing the collapse of many of the infrastructures we have used for our own lives. If those outer structures don't offer a bridge to the new way as they collapse and die off, that can make us feel hopeless and confused and insecure.

What's an answer? I know for sure one answer is the inward journey, and I'm passionate about helping people turn toward themselves. I'm passionate about, as Michael Beckwith says, the United States of Consciousness. I'm passionate about helping people understand the inner governance that is available to them. I'm here to help people recognize that, when they lose that outer structure of security, there is an inner structure of security that is always present. I'm here to help people understand that, back behind the conditions of their lives, there is always a non-physical cause. There's always a spiritual seed.

It does have to do with the New Way. It has to do with the new design that is seeking to emerge through whomever is making themselves available to it. That's what I'm inviting you to do today. I know that this is necessary for all of us, including these young people who are depressed and hopeless as they look into the world and wonder what the hell is going on.

Be mindful of where you might be placing your security and sense of self in the outside world and where these structures might be falling away, collapsing, and causing you concern and fear. And just be mindful that, oftentimes, things are falling away or dissolving as a prompt for something new to bloom, as a prompt to turn away from the world of affects and the conditions and turn back toward your heart and soul. Take a fine-tooth comb through your thinking and your belief system and assess what's true for you today and what may no longer be working for you. It takes a tremendous amount of guts and courage to step out of that and into your own thing.

There is hope. That hope lies in the center of your own beingness. There's something that's breathing you and beating your heart, something that orchestrates the cycles of the oceans, something that holds all the planets in place. There's some Intelligence that rises the sun and packs the rose into the seed. Something cracks that seed open and draws forth that bloom! And it's time that we tune into that and be available to It and receptive to It.

Day 69: Seeing the Truth of the Lie That Has Told Me I'm Not Enough

I've been wanting to get back into the world of men. It's taken me quite a while to take the leap. This year, it dawned on me that, no matter how many years I say, "Next year I'm going to have a man in my life," I never do; probably because just saying it is not enough. You have to actually intend it and take action steps. So I told a friend that I was ready to go join an online dating site. Even if I don't meet somebody there, it's a good way to move the energies forward in this area of my life. I gave myself a deadline to get my profile page up, which I did, and then I just browsed and dabbled for a while.

In my meditation today, as if I was watching a movie, I was seeing my reaction in the past when men would give me attention. My reaction had always been one of excitement, but also surprise. Then I was shown that one of the main reasons I've been surprised by such attention is because I have felt unworthy and unpretty, not "relationship material". It was a very tender experience and another moment where I simply had to totally love myself. I had to wrap my arms around the self that believed this and has been in pain about that all these years. I'm much better, now, at accepting how I look but a piece of that still lurks within me.

My mom, bless her heart, is very fixated on appearances and always has something to say about my hair or whether or not I'm wearing makeup. I've grown up with a sensitivity to appearances indicating worthiness. But I also lay some of that at the door of religion, which had me repeat things like, "Lord, I am not worthy to receive you," time and time again. I was told that I am only half until a man picks me, and then I am made whole. It's taken a long time to undo all of that. But today, in the vast space of my meditation, it was really profound to see so very clearly that my sense of unworthiness lets me to react with surprise when a man responded to me – especially if he was really handsome. As if I thought that who I am is not a match for a really handsome guy.

This is a tender revelation today. I need to be clear about who I am and authentic with the love that I have for myself. I need to see the truth, the beauty, the prettiness of who I am. Not because I'm comparing – compare and despair – but because I actually see it. I see the Divine. I see the Goddess. I want to be in complete alignment with who I am so that I can attract a man or men into my life who are in complete alignment with who they are.

This is about maturing. It's not necessarily an age thing; you can have this maturity at a young age. This is part of the maturity that comes with falling in love with myself, and it comes because I've made time to develop a relationship with myself. I've cultivated love and appreciation and enjoyment with and for myself, as I am. I am surprised that all this came up today, out of the blue. But that's the language of the Infinite, the language of the Universe.

Today I'm going to go back and get that young girl, that teenager and bring her home to my heart space. I need all of me to bring forward the great love of my life. I need my little self, my adolescent self, my awkward teenage self, and my powerhouse young adult woman. I want all of me to come home so we can go do this together.

Look in the mirror and really see the truth of who you are. Take some time and wrap your arms around yourself and tell yourself that you love yourself, and really mean it. Look in the mirror and keep looking until all you see is the Divine that breathes you, the Divine that clothes itself as you so it can come out and play.

Thirty one days to go. I have a feeling that 100 days won't be the end of this.

Day 70: The Old Skin Cannot Hold the New Wine

Last night I was writing and feeling some discontent around my identities and stories and the way things have been. I was looking at this woman, Danielle LaPorte, out of Vancouver. She's got a great rock 'n roll edge to her. She wrote a book called "White Hot Truth" and is on a book tour now. She has a very streamlined way of delivering her information. She's got one Facebook page and one Twitter account. I was thinking about how I have my personal Facebook page, the This Awakening Spirit Facebook page, and The Camille Conte Show Facebook page for my radio show. I've got two Twitter accounts. I've got camilleconte.com and This Awakening Spirit as separate websites. I'm not yet fully integrated.

While I was writing, I asked, "Do I need to let go of everything?" I realized that I was trying to take what already exists and integrate it into something new, one thing. Maybe the discontent is coming because I need to let it all go. At the very least, I need to clear the table and start anew. As much as my ego shouted, "Hell no!" to that and felt freaked out, I could also feel excitement. There was a freeing feeling around the idea of just being Camille Conte in the world. I want all these different ways in which I express myself to follow who I am, not be who I am. I gotta tell you, this is simultaneously scary as shit and exciting as all get out. This is what it's like to literally be on the edge and to leap. I don't know what it's going to look like, but I can feel it coming. This is the chrysalis phase moving into the experience of having wings.

When we deepen our awareness of the Self, when we consciously and co-creatively take on our own personal evolution, shift happens! We outgrow things and they fall away. The more

I change internally, the more the outer container has to change to match that which is new. The old skin cannot hold the new wine, as the saying goes. Maybe all of these containers that have held the Camille that has been in the world are no longer necessary. Maybe there's a singular container that's seeking to emerge and hold all of it. Like I said, there something unbearably exciting about all of that, but at the same time I'm thinking to myself, what the hell are you saying? The ego pipes up and says, *Do you understand what you're talking about? You just got business cards done!* All the stress really is from the ego mind. This is not to say that I won't continue to be these expressions, but I can clearly see that things are happening on a cellular level. I know how this works. The outer is falling away because it can't hold the new.

With 30 days left, I am committed to finishing my writing. Back when I was with the Flow Group in California, we imagined what things would be like 90 days in the future. One of the things I said was, "I didn't know this book was inside me and now I have this completed manuscript!" It felt so real.

And it is – it's the power of the spoken word. I called all of this forth, including a finished manuscript. I want to finish this so the journey and story is complete. This is the end. This is the end of the story from confusion to clarity. I think of the lyrics from that Who song, "The Real Me": *Can you see the real me? Can ya*?! It's bold to make space for a new self to emerge even if you don't have all the information yet.

Day 71: I Have No Idea What I'm Becoming

Today is a purposefully quiet day. I am still in a meditative state and listening deeply. I have put some specific questions out to the Universe, including, "Why am I passionate about the things that I'm passionate about? What is my Why, my driving purpose, for being on the earth – personally, and as a servant to humanity?" My ego mind keeps me distracted by presenting a slew of questions to me that create doubt, uncertainty, and confusion. Through meditation, I've been able to untangle myself and un-identify as that. I am no longer confused; however, I may experience confusion. Those are two completely different things.

I know my ego mind well enough to know that it takes tremendous mindfulness to make it ok for me to spend this next month getting this story down. I gave my word and I'm completing it to the best of my ability. But my goodness, my mind is just working overtime to keep me distracted from writing.

And, what's next? I don't know – I've never done this before. I can honestly say I really don't know what I'm about to become, and I'm fascinated by that comment. I'm excited to see what is being formed. I know it's happening! I've done enough personal work to have an awareness of my inner reconfiguration. I'm staying in the quiet place today, which is a really beautiful gift we can give ourselves. I hope that, in the busyness of your day, you can take some time to be still, whether it's for a few minutes or longer.

When I worked in the restaurant industry and was either exhausted or stressed out, I would escape into the bathroom for some quiet. I would stay there for several minutes until I could breathe normally and get centered. You can do the same. If you can go for a walk during a lunch break, do it. If all you've got is a bathroom where you can stare into the mirror and appreciate yourself and love yourself and breathe into an open heart, do that. When you leave work and you're in the car, chant some Oms or do some breathing. It helps dissolve the energy of the day so that you can wash away whatever no longer serves you. With all that's going on in the world of affects, the headlines, I invite us to remember that how we are feeling is important. We're here to feel joy. We're here to feel and experience love. We're here to feel the ease and flow of life as our very own. If it feels heavy, it's probably not what you're here to experience, though we've certainly been trained to believe that heaviness is exactly what we're here to experience. I would say, today, that is most definitely not true.

Day 72: I'm Letting Go of Who I've Known Myself to Be and My Ego is Freakin' Out

My meditation was beautiful today. I'm so filled up. I'm really proud of myself. This is one of the boldest and bravest things I've done. And what am I doing? I'm dying to the old and welcoming in the new. These last several days have been so personally deep. I look at the last four months and let me tell you something - these have been extreme life altering days.

This next chapter of my life is coming out of something else. Perhaps pieces of what was here before will be integrated into what is coming. But I'm letting go of these identities. I'm letting go of the attachments to how I've shown up in the world, and my ego is freaking out because my ego wants to be loved, seen, recognized, and be part of what's familiar. It wants to rest on the past, because it's familiar with that. And I'm calling in something bigger. How outrageous is that?

There's something in here waiting for my recognition. As I look back at this tapestry of my life, the pattern can't be seen up close. I have to step way back from the tapestry to see it in its entirety. This meditation experiment has been causing me to walk further and further away from the tapestry of my life. I was so engrossed in the individual threads that I was losing sight of the full picture. As I step further back and see the fullness of what's going on and the divine timing and divine unfoldment that's been going on since February, it's incredible! I want to write this story. This is important and meaningful.

Healing ourselves helps to heal others. When you do your own personal work and forgive and mend your own separation from yourself, when you go about falling in love with yourself and accepting your beauty and divine nature, you help yourself and everybody around you. Because there's only One Thing happening, and It's got the incredible, unbounded, infinite intelligence to become everything. It looks like there's more than one thing happening but that's the whole point; there isn't. There's just One Thing happening.

I'm fired up. Things are starting to emerge and make sense.

Day 73: When You've Outgrown Your Belief System, or Your "BS"

After my meditation this morning, I was looking at some of the notes I took while watching Michael Beckwith speak at Agape International. Some things really stood out to me and are in synch with my feeling-state after my meditation.

He said that a belief system is not going to help you after a while. It's the practice that leads to the personal experience. I've been working on my belief system since I was 18 years old, really. Then I got into Science of Mind and Spirit in 1991, and I aggressively stepped on to a spiritual education path that basically took me deep inside myself so that I could get face to face with my beliefs, my belief systems, how they were operating, what were inside them, whether or not they were still mine, and doing that wonderful, profound, and life changing work.

However, this idea that – after a while – your beliefs no longer serve you is totally resonating with me. All these years on the path, I've been stepping into my personal experience of the Thing Itself whether I realized it or not. Joel Goldsmith calls it "practicing the presence". Meditating for an hour everyday has put me into a place of personal experience and that is where it's at. Whoever you're inspired by or following, at some point you've got to begin your own practice so that you can have your own experience, your own revelations, and your own transformation.

I have made that leap from beliefs to experience myself. Michael Beckwith said something important about how that has helped him: "There's no way I could be doing what I'm doing, standing up in front of people and saying what I'm saying, if it was just my belief, just a theory, just a philosophy. It has to be coming from a personal experience." I just totally get that. You know what I'm saying? I know you understand that. As helpful as it is for you to learn from my experience or the experiences of others, the point is to have your own personal experience. That's the real deal.

This is a significant shift to dwell on, to understand our connection to Source and this idea that our needs are already met. So how am I going to act from that consciousness? Join me in thinking about this. Maybe pick one area of your life where you can consider that all of your needs are met. How would you feel? For me, it takes me out of the material and puts me completely into the spiritual. It takes me out of the world of affects and puts me into my own inner affects. It has my senses working not from the outside in, but from the inside out.

One of the ways I would be acting if I was truly coming from the consciousness that all of my needs were met would be peace. I'd have peace of mind, a calm certainty and an eagerness to see how it's all going to unfold, a welcoming through a mode of receptivity. This is something I've been dwelling on for the last 24 hours. If everything I desire is already done energetically in the invisible vortex of my life, then my role, as a creator, is to speak it as if it's already here, even though there's evidence that it's not, so that it has a bridge to cross over from the invisible to the visible. This is how creation works. It's this idea of receptivity. And of course, there are moments when doing-ness is absolutely necessary. However, having receptivity be your action step blows the roof off the joint. It completely takes everything we've ever learned and throws it upside down.

I'm stepping into this new experiment of being a receiver of the gift. I'm literally opening up my arms and my hands throughout the day. I'm receiving. You can give it to me. My arms, my heart, my mind, my consciousness. I'm open to receiving whatever it is that is seeking to emerge. The fullness of life is always seeking an outlet. It's always seeking that crack of least resistance, so I'm trying to widen that crack.

That's a little bit about what's going on with me today. I hope you take some time to open up your mind and your heart; open up your arms and your hand and receive the gift. If somebody tries to give you something today, just say, "Thank you." If you find yourself pushing it back or saying, "No" or doing anything like that, just stop. Say, "Thank you, yes. I will receive your help." Begin to get comfortable receiving. You deserve it.

Day 74: When I'm Looking at What Isn't, I Don't See What Is

Today I'm excited because I was shown an old, ingrained way of seeing things that I have not yet stepped out of. When I dwell on what isn't happening in my life, I cannot see what is there. Most of the time I don't know that I'm looking through that filter, which is why it's taken me this long to awaken to this important understanding. This is a practice. You have to keep swinging the hammer. You have to be willing to continue the old habit to see it, so that you can have a reference point to what no longer serves you.

I want to specifically talk about money. I had been looking only at one bank account for so long and what wasn't in it that I forgot I have another bank account. While I've been looking at this one bank account and it's dwindling numbers, I have also been affirming my flow and un-identifying myself with the dollars. I have been shifting my awareness, as I mentioned yesterday, to the feeling that all of my needs are met. Bank accounts are just numbers; they grow and then get small and then grow again. That's just the nature of what my experience has been, though an ever-increasing good is what my experience is right now.

In my meditation, I was shown that I have this whole other bank account. Then I found out this account has a sister credit union right where I'm staying. It has always been there. The money I need to buy a ticket to go back to Alaska has always been there. However, I was only able to see and remember it because I shifted my sights away from lack to being open enough so the money could show me where it was. I've often beaten myself up for my relationship with money. I've looked out into the world of affects and made that judgment about myself. But you know what? I'm in a very smart moment in my financial life. My choices are making this life of caring for my mom possible.

This is about being sourced by the One Life that lives and moves and has its beingness in, through, and around me. An ever-expanding good. That's heaven.

Day 75: Remaining Centered While the World Comes at You

It's so freaking hot today, about 95 degrees. I do not do well in this type of heat. Today's message is that it takes practice to not let the environment affect us. It takes practice, awareness, devotion, intention, and attention to not let the elements of our environment steal our joy or decrease our vitality. It takes practice.

Between the heat and conversations and interactions and all these different things that we call our daily living, today I am practicing the application of what I've been learning. I am in a heightened state of awareness because I'm aware that these elements and this environment can, if I let it, affect me internally. I'm strengthening my skill to not let that happen. I am strengthening my ability to be who I am, to stand in the vibration of love and peace, in the midst of exchanges with strangers who are really hot because it's 95 degrees and they don't know who to take it out on so they take it out on a stranger. To be the space that doesn't take that personally – it's a practice.

Don't let anybody fool you; I don't care how many retreats you go to or how many books you read. It's a practice to become aware and act consciously. Today I have had no shortage of opportunities to practice and strengthen my resolve to be centered, no matter what.

Day 76: 76 Trombones and the Agenda of the Ego Mind

One of the things that Michael Beckwith said in our meditation retreat was that the ego is merely unexamined perceptions, unexamined beliefs, and unexamined thinking. In my meditation today, I was in the front row seat, detached and observing my ego mind. I was looking with tremendous attention at what was troubling it and what it was consumed by. It comes down to things like separation, competition, being right, identity, comparing, and the jealousy, anger, righteousness. It's been a fascinating observation.

I had a difficult communication exchange with someone yesterday, and I watched my thoughts as the night unfolded. I watched how my ego mind held onto it and came up with script after script about what I was going to say. While it was doing that, I was simply choosing to observe it and not do anything except be mindful that this was the ego's agenda and my agenda is to love and try something different. I was observing the incredibly detailed scripts that my ego was laying out for me, making a really good case that I should call this person back, and this is what I need to say, and how dare they, on and on.

While there may be a time that I have to speak my truth about this (although I'm not feeling that coming anytime soon), it's really important not to use that as a cover-up for spewing anger or mean-spiritedness or any of those emotions that are based in separation. It's one thing to speak your truth and be calm and peaceful and loving – speaking from a slightly detached place – as opposed to barreling down on somebody. That happens in the human experience and, when it does, it's good to apologize when you see how you might have steamrolled over somebody.

But I digress. When I woke up this morning, I kid you not: it was as if my mind was just waiting for me to come into consciousness and there it all was again. I actually told it to go away and leave me alone. It just wouldn't stop. I knew that, when I got into my meditation, this exchange was going to be there. The power of the meditation time is my opportunity to observe my mind without identifying with it. To observe it without feeling that this is the necessary path for me to take. To observe it and understand that the ego mind presenting this is literally fighting for its life. This is why it comes up with these methods and scripts; it's fighting for its identity and it's fighting to be right.

In the wonderful book by Matt Kahn, "Loving What Is," he says to love whatever arises. He also talks about how to master relationships and how to bring love, actively and with words, to a situation where someone is clearly less than loving. He talks about how to respond in a way that represents the presence of love. I'm so fascinated by this. I've done it the other way most of my life, I've reacted to pain with my own hurt and anger. I'm tired of that. It doesn't work, and it keeps me in a low vibration which I have no interest in being in.

So how can I look at this situation and step outside of the ego mind? How can I bring love to this? How can I have a greater understanding or compassion? How can I allow the Presence to come through me and use me as Its vehicle? How can I allow It to emerge in my conversations and relationships as love?

This is where practice comes in. It takes courage and, really, a bit of strength to let go of the role that I've played in these intimate relationships and to really choose to be the place where love reveals itself. When you live from there, there's no room for anything else! You can only have one or the other. It's a practice. And thank goodness I have people in my life who are really allowing me to master this, because I want to. I don't want to continue doing it the way that I've been doing it all these years.

It's a goof that we can't see most of who we are. It's a trip that most of what is real is in the invisible realm. It's all energy. As Beckwtih says, it has to be seen with the Eye behind the eye and heard with the Ear behind the ear. And how does that happen? Through meditation and practice.

Day 77: You Want to Change the World? Wake Up to Your Own Magnificence

Today I am acutely aware of a truth that has been picking up momentum and speed inside me: if you really want to change the world, your country, your state, your community, or your relationships, the fastest way to do that effectively and with a depth of permanence is to wake up. People awaken in different ways. We wake up by being willing to take all the things we've learned, read, and know - all the workshops and counseling sessions - deep down. To take it all in and to put it into action.

How do we put it into action? There's got to be a daily commitment to spending time with yourself, however that looks. Some people have that connection when they're in nature. Some people simply get comfortable being with themselves (the inner self) and being willing to go through the chaos, confusion, family history, and attachments. To be willing to travel through it in awe, as an observer, until you come out the other side and see the glory, splendor, and magnificence of who you truly are.

This is not a religious thing. This is a truth. We are spiritual energy and spiritual essence having a material incarnation. We have filled ourselves up with the material education. This awakening happens when we take the inward journey and decide to add some things that connect us with the invisible realm, the spiritual realm, to spend some time connecting with the thing that's breathing you, the thing that beats your heart without any need for you to be involved at all. The Intelligence that has somehow clothed itself in this skin, bones, and flesh is truly magnificent. So take time to deeply appreciate your body and to contemplate the magnificence of this machine. Make a commitment to raise the vibration of the foods you take in, stepping away from processed food and choosing instead to eat from your local farmer whenever possible. Everything is a vibration.

And if you're finding yourself in a low vibration because of things happening outside of yourself, I encourage you to turn away. Go for a walk. Drink something with a lot of greens in it. Do something to raise your vibration and make yourself available to what's seeking to emerge through you, as the solution to your situation. You're here at this particular time for a particular reason. And yes, waking up can be intense, painful, and unbelievably messy. However, it can also be unbelievably joyful and awe inspiring.

The best way to change the world is to change your life and the best way to change your life is to wake up.

Day 78: I May Have Pushed Your Button, But I Didn't Install It

Not so long ago I heard somebody talk about emotional freedom. They talked about it from the context of not being emotionally triggered by what somebody was saying or doing or not saying or not doing. I was immediately inspired and excited by that possibility. From that point on, I have always held within myself a desire to master this and to experience emotional freedom, to get to a place where, no matter what was done or said, it wouldn't affect me because I was affected by my internal world. I was understanding that, whatever someone was saying or doing, was coming from their internal world.

I have a wonderful mentor in my life, Reverend Rainbow Johnson, who said, "I might have pushed your button, but I didn't install it." That's this idea that we're all walking around with file cabinets filled with pain bodies, as Eckhart Tolle would call them. The outer world is often triggering those pain bodies. People, places, things, circumstances, headlines: you name it. We get triggered and we have an internal, emotional reaction. Our ego mind tends to present that to us as if the person or thing outside of ourselves is the problem or cause. Consequently, we blame, we get angry, we have resentments, we have judgment, there's discord in relationships, and on it goes.

So I've been asking for insight to help me understand what it takes to be the revealer of love in every situation, particularly with our family. We tend not to talk about family stuff, right? But I think, at some point, somebody's got to talk about this because we all want harmony. We all want to be loved. We want to be seen. I think that the universal family is all craving the same thing. And yet, there's that one person – maybe it's you – in the family that has been called to be the healing agent, to be the one that is revealing love in every situation. I've come to realize that this requires us to truly not take anything personally, for starters. Part of my process of not taking anything personally is to witness myself taking things personally. The first process is to detach from identifying myself as being attacked and to just witness the self that feels attacked. That's a powerful shift, right there. Once I'm able to have that opportunity and really be in that place, I'm able to go back even further and be in the field of love while observing myself having a reaction. Once I'm able to dissolve that, I'm able to see the other individual's experience from the eyes of love and to realize that, whatever's coming from someone else is coming out of their internal experience.

This is really big. If you're in a relationship, if you've got a working or family relationship, you have this opportunity. A great book to read is the "The Four Agreements". I remember when I first read that book, I threw it across the room because I was so pissed off at it. It challenged everything I was told. Don't take things personally...are you kidding? I grew up being told that you should take everything personally. I grew up being told that everything was an affront and an attack, and how dare they?

The other thing is that if you're feeling called to be the one that reflects love, you have to take time for yourself. You have to unplug so you can get tuned in to the Self within you because that is the One that will be the revealer of this love. But, even still, I can't do this on my own. I was like, *Look: I want to be the place where this love expresses itself. I want to be the channel through which this mighty and powerful energy that I call love has a place to emerge and come through.* That's my relationship to It, that's how I talk to It.

I'm thinking about the man who went on a shooting spree at the UPS office and the man who went on a shooting spree at the ballpark this June. I'm thinking about the man who stabbed people on the train, and all the acts of violence that we don't know about. Inside each one of those people is the same divine expression that is inside you and me. When we see It in ourselves, we eventually have the opportunity to see It in another. Perhaps that's something you'll consider today.

Day 79: A New Way to be in Our Relationships

I wanted to talk a little bit more about this new way of being. One of the things that's true for me is that I'm able to see the process. The process, at first, was that I was on the merry-go-round inside the circus of my thoughts. After a while, I was able to release myself from the nucleus of that insanity and move toward the edge where I was able to begin to have the observer's view. As time went on, I was able to detach from that ball of confusion that was my thoughts, and really solidify my observer's perspective. As that strengthened, I was able to disentangle myself from my thoughts which allowed me to no longer identify myself *as* them. So it became, "I'm feeling sad," versus "I AM sad."

As I continued to pull back from it all and ended up sitting from the Divine's perspective, I came to realize the other great gift of meditation. My initial identity was with the ego mind and I then reached the space in between the ego mind and the Mind behind it. This allowed me to see my true identity. For me, our true identity is the divine essence, that spiritual seed within each of us. This idea that much of who we are is invisible is why meditation and other spiritual practices are so important. They help connect you with that unseen, and yet, very real world. When we talk about being in relationships in a new way, it begins with this identity and this new self-absorbed, self-realized, self-experiencing identity that

I would call Spirit, Divine, God, or whatever the word is for you. It's the feeling-state of being the essence of Life itself. As you begin to be in that essence and as you begin to practice seeing yourself as that Presence, that becomes your identity and who you are.

Next, decide that you're going to be of service. This was a huge thing that happened for me a few weeks ago when my colleague and I were going through an interesting experience and I was having an ego reaction, an emotional reaction, to what people were saying. He said, "I'm here to be a healing presence. Whatever's going on for them that's being projected on me, that's theirs. I'm here to heal." That really struck me because I knew it was a high calling, I knew it was higher than where I was, and I knew it was a place I wanted to reach toward. In the weeks that have since passed, I've had plenty of opportunities to really appreciate the depth of this choice: I'm here to be a healing presence.

When you take that on, you're no longer a daughter or a partner or a friend; you take on a new role. What is the skill of that new role? To listen deeply. How can you sit there and listen to people talk in a negative way about you? First, because you know the truth of who you are. Secondly, you're no longer taking things personally, so you understand that's all inside them and it's being projected on you. You can recognize that this isn't about you; they're in pain. They're seeking love. They're seeking relief from their pain. As the healing presence, you are going to offer the space where, perhaps, that will happen for them by simply listening.

This is a new way. I'm in the midst of practicing this. I have by no means mastered this. I had a really tremendous swing into it the other day and was fired up. A few hours afterward, I swung back into a deep sadness. I simply allowed that to happen. I allowed tears to burst out of my eyes while I was washing dishes, because I was feeling pain and sadness, myself. When you're awakening, it's totally natural for all that's heavy and in the darkness to come up because you're shining the light on it.

When that happens, you have to love yourself, hold yourself, be gentle with yourself, and simply allow it. Just love it and love that part of you that's having that painful experience, because that's exactly the role that you are strengthening.

The ending is important here, because the practice includes being available for yourself when you're in pain, when emotion is coming through you, to listen to the self that's in pain and to simply allow that pain to come through you. As you learn how to do that for yourself, you're going to have a much easier time of being able to do that for another. This is the new way. This is how we heal our lives, this is how we heal our relationships, this is how we become a healing presence for this world. Based on everything I'm seeing, we need as many healing presences as we can muster.

80: The Father Within Doeth the Work

This is Day 80! There was a time when I was wondering when this freaking crazy experiment was ever going to end, and now – of course – I don't want it to. And isn't that the way they say it goes? What came through me today in meditation was the Father within doeth the work. A pretty appropriate message for today, Father's Day.

Last night, I drove down to Asbury Park to see Willie Nile, and I had a really wonderful time. Prior to that, I met up with a friend who's known me for 50 years. We had a wonderful conversation and we were sharing some of the experiences we find ourselves in. Even though we haven't been in touch for a while, it was remarkable how similar they were. We've always been slightly on the edge, the ones who forsook the traditional way of doing things to carve out our own path. I felt understood.

On the drive home, I had a full on conversation with The One. It was wild. I wish I was able to tape it. I just allowed myself to say all the things I needed to say to It. One of the things that became really clear was that I cannot stuff the genie back in the bottle. Something significant has happened to me in these

80 days. Things have changed. Things have been exposed to me in ways that I've never seen before. I simply can't undo what's been done. What is seeking to emerge does not have a past. That makes it very uncomfortable for my ego self and, sometimes, just for myself because I have no reference point.

So, this is active faith. I know something is changing, I know I've been changing, I know a fuller integration is happening, I know that transformation is going on, and I know that something is coming and I don't know what it is. Of course, I want to know as that would bring some peace of mind to my heart. The new opportunity is to bring peace of mind to my heart even in the absence of what I think I need to have to have peace of mind.

As I drove, I kept talking to the Divine about going back and forth from Alaska to New Jersey and being of service to my mom and trying to figure out what I'm doing. At that point, it became so clear to me that the Father within doeth the work. In other words, this, of myself, I can't do. I have taken this thing as far as I can take it. It's not to say I'm devoid of choices or that I don't have an active role in what's going on. I'm so far gone in this experience and experiment that there's no turning back. I can't get answers and figure stuff out the old way. It's about this deeper surrender and collaboration with what is seeking to emerge.

So today, the Father within doeth the work. Father, Mother, God, whatever the word is. It's not the word "Father"; it's the idea behind the word Father, The Thing within me that knows, The Thing that's put this physical outfit on Itself and named Itself Camille – that is the thing within that is doing this work. And what is my role? Well, my role is to trust, to have faith, to ask what's mine to do and then do it.

My heart is wide open. I'm thinking about my father on this Father's Day. I miss him. My dad passed onto me in my DNA the gift of being an entertainer. He was, in the highest sense of the word, an entertainer. He was a phenomenal drummer and singer and band leader and showman. I am those things too. I celebrate him today by celebrating what he's passed on to me.

The Father within doeth the work.

Day 81: I Failed Miserably at Being the Change I Want to See in the World

Yesterday I failed miserably at being the change I want to see in the world. It was a stressful and emotionally draining day, which caused me to be unable to sleep last night, which has not made today a day where I feel at my best. My nervous system was overstimulated and I allowed myself to go emotionally off the rails. I can feel that today, kind of like a hangover without the alcohol.

The four approaches I'm practicing and bringing to my relationships are:

1. Identify myself as the presence of love. I'm not a daughter, I'm not a sister, I'm not a friend. My role has changed.

2. I'm not taking anything personally. I have a deeper understanding that people's pain can be projected outward and seemingly be about me. However, by not taking things personally, I can do the third step.

3. Be a healing presence. The best way I can accomplish this is to move to the fourth step.

4. Deeply listen.

Where I tripped up yesterday was with taking things personally and being a healing presence. It's unfortunate that I had to go through that again to get yet another reminder of what it is I'm not wanting to do anymore and who it is that I'm not wanting to be. I just wanted to be honest with you about that because mastery comes with the practice, and I'm certainly going to have more opportunities to try this again.

I can tell, for sure, that the big piece here, is the me that clung to being righteous and right, that clung to being in the ego mind with its filter of separation and right and wrong and good and bad and evidence and proving. I've outgrown it, that's what it feels like. It feels like much of me has outgrown this way of behaving and now I'm waiting for the rest of me to join the new way.

Family dynamics and friend dynamics and co-worker dynamics are the core relationship dynamics that we have around us. They're there so that we can decide what is ours to do and which way we're going. Finding your center, identifying healthy boundaries, and choosing which way you want to go on all of this is the new way. It's not the easiest way, but it certainly is the new way.

Day 82: Our Individual and Collective Nervous System is Over-stimulated

I didn't really feel like making this video today, but I did it anyway. I've been releasing a lot of tears and just recently was able to calm down enough to roll tape. I've been thinking about my adrenals and my central nervous system because it's overstimulated and I think that, collectively, our central nervous system is overstimulated as well.

On a collective scale, there's just too much heavy duty information coming at us too fast. It's non-stop and nobody can keep up with it. Each and every story feels like it's of such magnitude that people aren't processing it. It's stressing people out. Personally, it feels very similar. There is a lot of information coming through my life right now.. I'm leaving on July 7th to go back to Alaska and my mom is already very emotional about that, as am I. Family dynamics are what they are.

I've been talking a little bit about how to be the change in our relationships and I was watching Michael Beckwith's talk from Wednesday of last week. He was saying, when we have a problem, it's not about God coming down to solve our problems;

it's about us moving closer to God, where our problems dissolve. In the Christ Consciousness, in that moment of awareness, in the full expression of love, there are no problems. That was really impactful to me. When we have problems going on in our lives, not only is it an opportunity to move closer to this thing we sometimes call God, it's also an indication that change is on the way. This is an interesting concept to dwell on. I'm looking at my problems now through the lens of growth, of change.

Day 83: Why Are We So Afraid to Feel Our Feelings?

The last several days have been emotionally challenging and draining. I said to my beloved colleague today, "I'm in a situation that requires me to lift 500 pounds, and I can only lift 100. I'm in way over my head."

He said, "Ah. You know what you need? You need a spotter." I said, "You're right. I do need a spotter." Of course, then he said, "Do you know who your spotter is?" And I do. The God of my understanding, the Love Intelligence that is present though I cannot see It. So, yet again, I am turned more deeply toward myself and the light within. As we go toward the light, the Presence, and the love, the problem doesn't have to be solved because it dissolves.

For me, there's no place to go but toward myself. I have so radically changed; everything that once was no longer is, and to such an incredible degree. I know there's nothing outside of myself, so the only thing I can do is to keep turning back toward myself and to keep going deeper. It's a good thing this Presence is unbounded and inexhaustible and infinite, because just when you think you've gone in as far as you can go, lo and behold – you've got to go deeper. And so, I do.

My beloved friend Sacha did a very brave, and truthful video the other day where she talked about feelings and how we've been trained to not feel, but rather to be numb. We've been trained to take the edge off through denial, drugs, alcohol, sex, food, exercise, adrenaline activities – the list goes on. We're so afraid to feel. We're so afraid to feel that we actually believe that other people are causing how we feel. We want them to have said things differently and to have done things differently so that we would have felt differently. I've definitely mastered this avoidance and I'm unlearning that. I'm unlearning a lot of things.

In this effort of mine to be the healing presence of love, to not take anything personally, and to listen with compassion. I can see that there's a part of me that's not there yet. In these personal exchanges, I saw the need to defend. It was a back and forth. "I didn't say that, I didn't mean that." I saw the need to be right and correctly defined rather than to simply be a healing presence and not take anything personally, because it's not mine to take. In a way, I'm glad this change isn't happening instantaneously. The slowed down experience of me being gradually able to lift this weight is really important for my evolution and my growth.

I would say I'm in between two worlds. Before this, I was in the old world seeing the new world. Now I'm in between the two. I would imagine, after some time here, I'll eventually be in the new world. Meanwhile, today, I wish everybody I knew was here. I wish my friends were coming by to say hi and go out for coffee. I wish they were giving me hugs; but, they're not. I miss my friends. So I have to turn toward the One that's always here. I know I'm not alone. The more I see It, the more real It is. The more I turn toward It, the more It turns toward me.

Day 84: Do You Know How to Take Care of Yourself?

Caretaking. I'm thinking about how we take care of ourselves. Do we know how to take care of ourselves? I only recently learned how to take care of myself, in 2008, after my father's death, the end of my personal relationship, the end of my business partnership, my dog's death, and being fired from my job. This all happened in 8 month's time. It was definitely the darkest time of my life and I was like the walking dead. It was because of that complete annihilation, that complete death, that I learned how to take care of myself.

It began with basic questions, like "What do you need?" I would say, "Water." Then I'd go get myself water. That's how severe it was. But that was the beginning of a remarkable learning opportunity for me because I had learned how to take care of everybody else – and I know I'm not alone in that. Especially, as women, we have a huge ancestral role with caregiving. We have not learned how to take care of ourselves. We often feel guilty when we take time for ourselves, constantly feeling like we have to justify it. That's why I love doing these retreats for women about the transformative power of self-care.

Whether you're a man or a woman, the point is, ask yourself: "What do I need?" Ask yourself that question, and give yourself what you identify. Need a hug? Wrap your arms around yourself. Need to sleep? Lay down and take a nap. Need some air? Get up from the desk and take a little walk. Learn how to ask yourself what you need and then learn how to give it to yourself with total self-love and without any concern about how it lands for anybody else. It's a big deal to learn how to take care of yourself, especially if you're taking care of other people.

As parents, my gosh – that's such a big roll. Taking care of kids, of your spouse, of friends, of aging parents; whatever it is, taking care of other people is important, but it must come with the balance represented in that one fantastic direction: put the oxygen mask on yourself first before administering care to others. Right now, I'm going to practice self-care by making myself a grand bowl of cereal while watching one of my favorite shows, Chopped, to see if I can learn something new tonight.

Day 85: You Are Complete Already

I did just finish my meditation and I'm not quite sure what's going to be said as this tape rolls this morning. Something is breaking open inside of me yet again. It's pretty remarkable that I've been in front of this camera for 85 days. Though

I have "gotten used to it", it's still not my preferred way because there's something additionally vulnerable about somebody seeing your face and your facial expressions and being able to look into your eyes.

As I approach the end of my 100 day experiment, I have to look back again. There have been many significant changes. One of the changes is around alcohol. If this is going to be an authentic sharing, I have to be real about what I haven't said yet – I haven't had any alcohol in over a month. There was no alcohol at the meditation with Rev. Beckwith and coming out of the retreat I was sick with all the internal healing coming through me. This refrain from drinking has been organic. Organic endings are the best because they just happen.

I had been saying to myself for at least a year that I knew that there were certain habits in my life that, though I loved them and seemingly enjoyed who I was while doing them, my soul was saying, *In order for you to really go deeper and to expand your consciousness, this stuff is going to have to be released.* I've known that, but I haven't wanted to take action to release those habits. So this personal walk has included that knowledge while still choosing those habits. But now I'm witnessing the falling away of those habits without even thinking about them.

And this is all fluid. It's really hot right now and I am thinking an ice-cold beer would be amazing. I'm not saying I'll never have an ice-cold beer again. That's not the point. Only we know, only you know, only I know the personal truth of our own experiences. Then we do our best to explain it to people. But mostly, it's just something that people see. They see a change in our face, they see a change in the clarity in our eyes. Maybe we've lost weight. That's another thing that's happened for me. I'm down to 138 pounds, which is just happening without me pushing or trying. There's nothing I have to do or accept or push away. It's just an observational moment of, huh! OK. That seems to no longer be in the mix.

Two weeks from today I'm going back to Alaska. I always have anxiety when I leave my mom and go back to Alaska. So we're preparing for that. I'm going back to Alaska without any expectations this time around. I'm just right here, right now, in the moment.

This is further evidence of transformation, moving from the material into the spiritual. When you're in the material, you think that's where it begins and ends. We come from a place of asking questions like, "How do I make this work? How do I fix this? How do I solve this?" There's this idea that you've got to beat the pavement and make huge efforts because you're coming from the material world. When you begin to journey to the spiritual world where all your needs are met and you recognize yourself as a spiritual being that's perfect, whole and complete, the questions become, "What do I have to give? How can I be of service? What's seeking to emerge through me?"

It's a powerful shift in the relationship that I have, not just with myself, but with the Thing that breathes me. It's certainly not a common way of being. When you're not putting in effort or doing it in the way that we've been trained to do it, the ego has concerns. The other day, my ego was like – *Wow. Maybe you're not hustling enough. Maybe you need to hustle and get out there more and do this or that.* For a while I thought this might be true. Maybe I lost my hustle. It was an interesting thing to observe. But for sure, at this point, I can't go back into the world that's collapsed. It's not there. I can't go back into the me that's dissolved into becoming what she's becoming, because that version of Camille is no longer there.

The only thing I can do is to lean in, be patient, love myself, and to keep my practices active and a focal point in my everyday living. That's the best gift I can give myself – keep leaning in. Keep meditating. Keep praying. Keep reaching out to those who are aware of this journey that I'm on. Keep loving myself. Keep playing. Keep having fun. Keep being right now. Here. Not in the past, not in the future, but present right now, because in the right now, the breath exists complete, as does the answer to all of my needs.

It's such a significant shift to understand and really believe that all of my needs are met already. The bloom is already in the seed. The seed doesn't have to go do anything. The seed doesn't have to go make anything happen. It's already in the seed. All the seed needs to do is yield to the bloom. That's life-changing. I'm yielding to my bloom.

Day 86: The Road Less Traveled

Last night I joined some high school classmates at a barbecue. Some of these people I haven't seen in 37 years. It was wonderful to listen to them tell their stories and talk about my life in Alaska. Most, except me, took the path where they got married, had children and went to work mostly in Manhattan. Some of them divorced and remarried. One has a wife who had a stroke 10 years ago and it was really touching to watch him lift her up out of the car and into her wheelchair and to then lift her up from the wheelchair and into a lounge chair. It was a beautiful demonstration of love.

As I sat listening to everyone, I had a lot of compassion for how the system was failing them. Work at the same place, get married, have kids was a formula that we were all told to follow. We didn't know it at the time, but we were the last generation to be given those specific instructions that included getting a good job, working at one place for as long as possible and pouring your time into your work. Be loyal. This was the roadmap that was suppose to give us a successful life, a life that had security. That security was a golden carrot. It wasn't just going to be security in the present moment; following this formula was also going to give you security in the future because you were going to get your pension or retirement or IRA. I watched these beautiful people, who devoted their lives to that system, share stories of not been treated well by it. It's scary that they're having such difficult times.

It made me realize again, in a very acute way, that in the midst of the sharing and all the laughter and memories, I have taken the road less traveled. Work, lifestyle, relationship, security, I was most definitely realizing just how different my life is compared to others. I also realized that to do so, to live this authentic life fueled by my creative expression, my spiritual journey has been key. This is an important and an often-missed education. It's the missing piece that makes all the difference especially when it comes to making changes and doing new things.

Through this spiritual education, I've learned who I am and whose I am. We often think we are what we do but I've come to experience another identity. I have an eternal identity. I have a spiritual identity. No matter how bad it's gotten, at least I've been able to reach in and rest on that sense of self. This is why so many people take their own life when they lose their job because they've lost who they believe themselves to be. Even though I've had profound losses that have challenged my identity, deep inside I know who I am. That's the only real security.

This is what we're waking up to. This is what's collapsing, this false belief in a security outside of ourselves. There's no security there because you can't control what's outside of you. The only thing you can control is your own life, growth, and awakening. So even though I don't have many of the material things this path offered, I just feel like my consciousness is my security and that, no matter what is going to happen, I'm going to be OK. I am OK. I already know that all my needs are met. I open up my heart, hands, and mind to this knowing and say, "I'm willing to receive the gift that's already been given."

On Friday, I was asked to go to my mom's senior center because somebody passed. The woman who runs the center wanted me to come help with the ceremony. It was a privilege to look at these beautiful seniors and say what was on my heart and to talk about mourning, the importance of ritual, and making grief and loss OK. It was amazing. Many people came up and thanked me, or said, "I'm so inspired by your thoughts," or "Thank you for saying what you said," or, "What a gift you have."

We all have gifts. So take the time to connect with the identity within you. When you learn to love the mystery of life, when you realize that the heart wants to stay wide open even in the face of somebody's pain, you understand that you're the one to hold the vibration of love and peace in your relationships. When you choose these things, you MUST wrap your life around your spiritual practices, whatever they may be.

Today I'm just grateful. Thirty years in Alaska this summer, and here I am reconnecting with people from New Jersey that I haven't seen in 37 years. Why is this my life? Because I've taken the road less traveled. I wouldn't give it up for anything in the world.

Day 87: Here Comes Your 19th Nervous Breakdown

I avoided doing this video all day today because it hasn't been a good day for me, emotionally. I'm going to take a wild stab at this. I don't know if the meditation is loosening up hardened, hidden, emotional pain, or if the current situation is just causing fresh pain. I don't know which it is. I think today was a little bit of both, but certainly it seemed like something came unhinged and the something, of course, would be me.

I witnessed myself being extremely upset about something that's been going on for a very long time and something I've been trying to fix. I've been trying to fix a relationship, and I can't. I'm saddened by that. It feels a little bit like a failure. As I say that, I hear my heart say, *Hey, don't ever give up on things like this.* Maybe my approach has to change from the outer manipulation of people, places, and things, to perhaps a more modern and mature and current day approach, which might include more prayer and more personal work. I can definitely see that I have some post-traumatic pain that goes way, way back to my childhood.

I have a lot of grief over my mom. She's still here, but every day I notice that her memory is a little more challenged. I think back to when I was in Alaska in April, before I came back to

Jersey in May. I was with some friends, and one of the new people I met is a healer and was doing the Alexander technique on my arms. All of a sudden, my heart just burst open. A flood of tears came out of no place from nothing and I heard a voice say, *Spend time with your mom while she knows who you are.*

My ego believes that I need to understand why I had that very severe meltdown today. I really don't have to know. I have to take care of myself. I have to be willing to examine this and maybe even get some help, because some big stuff got unhinged today. This is a tough walk for me right now. I feel like it's difficult to be the change I want to see in my family, to be the loving essence, to be the vibration of peace and harmony, because there's a part of me that's been capsized and I gotta go rescue her before I can be anything for anybody else.

This is Day 87, and as the Rolling Stones sing, "Here comes your 19th nervous breakdown. You better stop, look around, here it comes."

Day 88: Bring the Little One Home to Your Heart

I want to see if I can describe a process that I offer my clients. It's the opportunity to go back and get our small self. I'll explain it in terms of me doing it for myself.

I recognize that I have this little Camille that was left behind, this young Camille who is showing up now as an emotional, energetically active representation of the times when I abandoned myself or pushed part of myself away. She is popping up in the way I talk about, react to, or hurt over things happening now. I need to bring her back to my heart so she and I can be integrated and this separation between us healed.

To do so, I get into a meditative state and then allow myself to remember where I mostly saw this little Camille. What room of the house? Where was she more often than not? I go into that room or area and sit down with her and make myself available to her. I say things like, "I'm so sorry it took me this long to remember to come back and get you, but now I'm here to listen to everything you have to say." Oftentimes that little person does have a lot to say. They talk about how difficult things were or have been. It's a powerful experience. It may sound a little "woo-woo", but I've had nothing but remarkable and miraculous results when I do this with clients or myself.

You stay with yourself until the past version of yourself has said everything they need to say. You continue to apologize for what they had to go through. You speak compassion to that little person as if they were right there in front of you. When you feel complete, you see yourself asking that little boy or girl if they're ready to come home. You tell them how important they are for this part of the ride and how much you need them and their spirit and their innocence. You tell them you can't go on without them, they're that important, and you're going to protect them and take care of them and you're not going to let these things happen to them again. In essence you are assuming the role of parent.

Then you put your arms out in front of you, lift them up in your mind's eye and bring them right into your heart. Literally move your hands towards your heart until they rest there. Take a deep inhale and exhale and really feel that little one there and really see them nestled at the center of your heart. Sometimes they want to bring something from the room with them. I've had moments where my little girl wants to bring a favorite stuffed animal. Whatever it is, don't judge it. Nobody has to know what you're doing.

Do this as many times as you have to. Do this for as many of your selves that are left on the side of the road. Go back and "get them" following the same procedure. I'm doing this for myself tonight and I'm looking forward to it because I want to use this opportunity to offer myself the same healing I offer my clients.

Day 89: Enlightenment is Not About the Absence of Difficult Times

I was on the phone yesterday with my roommate from the Agape meditation retreat, Jen Carlson, who is a very talented digital marketer and advertiser. We're bartering some services with each other, and I wanted her to take a look at everything I have because I think I have too much, as I've mentioned. Two websites, three Facebook pages, and two Twitter accounts. I look at some other people who have one of everything, all of their offerings aligned, and I want to do that as well. So I've asked Jen to help me and look at everything I have and give me some thoughts about it.

We were talking yesterday, and she said, "I'm going to send you some questions that I send all my clients because it's important to know what your message is." And boy, did that just ring true for me. What is my message? I thanked her for that and said, "Wow, maybe this is something I have to understand." She said, "Yeah, this is about you being the brand." It's taken me all these years to really feel comfortable with that. I've never liked being the focus; it was usually just the radio show's name like, "Cutting Edge with CC" or whatever I was doing that had the focus. But I've come to understand that this is something to embrace and consider, especially if I'm going to have an impact and help a large group of people. This is a template that works so I need to give it a try.

After we talked, I started thinking about this. I went into meditation again last night and I fell asleep as a result of it, which was great. But I went in asking, "What is my message? What is the message that gets expressed through me in my radio work and my public speaking and my one on one, through my classes and workshops? What is the message?" So this morning I had my meditation and I did my prayer call with my colleague. As we were in the midst of our heightened awareness, I heard a voice say, "You are the message." Ok, then. Problem solved. This is what happens with meditation. This is what it's like, the subtle healing of separation between asking the question and waiting for the answer, to asking the question and being the answer.

Yesterday I was believing, thinking, seeing it from the perspective that there is a message outside of me. As if I don't know what it is or that it's at a distance from me or is outside of me. So when I asked myself, "What is my message?" I can see now that I was asking from a pre-conceived belief that it was something I didn't know and had to get. Today I realized I am the message. I am the Thing itself. There's nothing to do but rather be. Do you know what I'm saying? This is the healing that's available to us. We think that everything is outside of ourselves. I still encounter this in myself, and though I'm someone who comes from a belief where I know that things are within, I can still have these subtle moments where an aspect of my thinking and my belief system relies on answers being outside of myself. So getting the hit that I am my message was a really exciting revelation to me. Also to note, it came as a feeling. As soon as I heard that voice while my friend was praying and doing his thing, my whole body lit up. I could feel it and I knew that was a sign, that this is Truth. I am the message.

Something has changed so profoundly and so deeply inside of me. Identities have fallen away so completely as I have become more aligned with my true identity and divine self, even though these last several weeks I've been in the human experience big time. This is an opportunity to be aware of the process of the human giving way to the divine. Enlightenment, for me, has never been about the absence of these difficult times or these challenging relationships. Enlightenment is being in the presence of these situations with a heightened awareness and a deeper self-love. It's about being able to love the me that is still dealing with the situation. It's about being able to hold myself and hold a space for myself so that a healing can come through and be felt. It's about identifying with the I Am. I am that I Am.

I've never read the Bible, but I have some awareness of some of the quotes from the Bible through the metaphysical lens. One of the things that really struck me today is that the promise is one of renewal. This is a significant promise today, and it's not just a promise. It's a probability and a real thing. That renewal is available to me, no matter what has happened to me, no matter what I've done or said, no matter what the conditions are around me, no matter the conditions of my relationships, no matter WHAT. No matter how cemented it appears, no matter how long it's been going on for. There is always an opportunity for renewal, for something to be reset, because we're dealing with a Power and a Presence that can rearrange conditions. It's greater than anything that I have been dealing with or am in the midst of, including this identity piece.

I appreciate every aspect of the human journey. I appreciate and have deep respect for the complete and total breakdown that I had that night in California and the emotional mess that I spilled all over the place because I am on the other side of that now with a greater awareness and the renewed hope to not give up on myself. To not give up on the promise of renewal. So I'm just really grateful I haven't abandoned myself or this experiment. I want to encourage you to stick with it, whatever it is you're going through and whatever it is that's going through you, stay with it. Love it. Hold it. Examine it. Reach out and get some help to support yourself as you move with it because something is happening. Something is becoming unhinged. Something is being brought to the light so that a greater expression can be revealed to you and you have the choice to go with it or not.

There are certainly moments when the updraft of renewal and transformation is so profound and you've yielded to it so completely that it takes you up without any effort on your part. I call it grace. Suddenly, the things that you've been holding onto for dear life... your hands just open up because this thing is pulling you and these other things just fall away. Yes, there can be grief and loss as a result of it, but what it's calling you forward and what it's bringing you to, and what it's revealing through you and what is emerging, is so much bigger. It's so real.

I am grateful for this journey. When I started, I never would've thought that this is where I'd be on Day 89. How could I have known? But the fact that I said yes and that I've continued to do it, no matter how much I've hated it along the way, no matter how long I've put off posting a video until night time, the fact that I'm here today and sharing this with you is really extraordinary. I hope there's something in here that resonates with you and helps you. I always love to hear any comments you share and what's happening for you as well.

Today, I renew myself. Today, I unhook myself from what's happened. I don't have to continue to feel badly about the way I behaved. It happened. It was. I am not doing anybody any good by remaining in that remorseful, low vibration state. I have a new awareness of what's happened, and I'm choosing to go to a different place. I'm choosing to rise up out of it. This is allowable. It's OK to do it! It's OK to completely fuck up and then have an awareness of what happened, communicate that to yourself and anybody else involved, and then rise out of it! That's the journey. And the ego mind is the only thing that would want to keep us prisoners to what was. It's the heart and the soul and the spirit that are always calling us toward what Is. Soul-ar energy. The source within, through, around, and as you and me. One thing happening.

Day 90: You Already Know What You Need to Know. You Just Might Not Know that You Know It

Ten days to go. That's remarkable. I had a lovely meditation this morning, just nice and peaceful. Toward the end these purple blobs come across my eyes, and I always feel like I'm spinning around in the stuff of the Universe right about that time. I'm certainly going to be continuing this meditation. I think I will continue sharing via video, but I don't know if it will be every day. We'll just see. It's nothing I'm feeling any need to know. Imagine that. I just don't need to know today about that which is 10 days from now.

In my meditation, I was asking for any insight about my trip to Alaska. I leave on the 7th and am feeling into things while I'm up there, ways in which I can teach or share what this journey has been for me. Things are starting to coagulate in a way that's giving me some insight and ideas. Everything is so different. I'm not the same person that I was when I left Alaska. I'm looking forward to the quiet that is Alaska and to the sacred energy that comes from that land.

Today I experienced a quiet grace. A quiet gratitude. I'm not really exploding with insight or deeply moved by something specific to share or to say to you or myself, for that matter. Maybe it's because all I did was to call forth to just be an expression of love, for myself and everyone around me. Sometimes that in and of itself is the practice. It always is enough. Loving ourselves first. I grew up thinking that was selfish. Turns out, it's the most important thing I can do for myself and you. Once you do that - you don't even have to master it - but once you start practicing loving yourself exactly as you are, warts and all as they say, the expression of love has a bigger channel through which to flow. That's how self-love is a selfless act. Besides, I certainly love this truth that you can't perfect that which is already perfect so just love It.

I was listening to this guy's webinar last night and he was talking about this wave that's coming and how to prepare yourself to catch the wave as an entrepreneur. As I was listening to him talk, he kept saying the words, "I promise you," over and over. I understood what was under that, but the more I heard him say that I kept thinking, *You really can't promise any of this.* I mean, how do you know? You only know from your own experience. I get that we want to be able to promise outcomes and we want to see for another the experience we are having, but there's nothing that you can truly promise. Though I did say yesterday, the promise is one of renewal, I think that comes from the only kind of promise that we can talk about which are the promises that are built on universal principles. We didn't create them and we can't un-create them. They exist. They're part of the scientific realm of our spiritual/material living.

But as this guy was talking he was clearly setting it up as a selling of his knowledge, as most of these people do. And that's fine, because I came through that myself and I'm on another side of it now. He was setting it up as, "I have information that you don't have. If you pay me $2,000.00, I'm going to give you the information that you need to be able to catch this wave and deliver your message to the world and make a generated income yourself. And maybe then you'll even be able to charge other people $2,000.00 to tell them what you think they don't know that you now know that they need to know."

It's an interesting thing. Meanwhile, there's Kyle Cease, who I so love, who doesn't do any of this. He doesn't send emails. I'm sure he creates an email list, but all he ever does is give away free content. He's just sharing his day-to-day experience. He's deeply resonating with people all over the place. Tens of thousands of people are watching his videos and responding on his Facebook page and sharing their transformative experiences and the changes and shifts that they're having. Then he goes out and does these events.

That's who I am right now. It's not to say that I'm not here to charge for my work, but I don't want to be a part of something in which I'm posturing myself as knowing something that somebody else doesn't know. There's just something about that that made me very stressed out. The two years in which I was involved in those moments, watching all these free webinars, giving my email address, getting on all these emails that come non-stop every other day, trying to figure out how to get the money to buy the course so I could learn what this guy learned so I could have the success that he had – for me, it was so stressful. In the end, it hasn't been something I want to be a part of long term, because the problem is that you can be in a perpetual wheel of thinking that you don't know what you need to know. You can keep buying all these courses, but you never get to the doing part.

That might just be my experience. I did take a course that was $997 and I learned a ton of stuff and did apply it. I'm not saying that they're completely invalid. I'm just trying to be in a different relationship with how I'm doing this. How does my soul want to be a part of this world of marketing and packaging and advertising? I just noticed that something that resonated so strongly with me last year just didn't resonate with me last night. And that's fine; maybe it will resonate with me tomorrow or in a year. But last night, it didn't. It's important to honor how we feel about things. For me, my feelings are my guide. They're my GPS. If something lights me up and makes me feel happy and wonderful, I go toward that. If something is heavy and doesn't make me feel good, I don't go toward it. Go toward what lights you up and makes you feel good, makes you feel better. Go toward what makes you happy. We think we have to hang out with these low vibration people or relationships or jobs or conditions. We don't. You're free to change your mind and your emotional state. You're free to forgive yourself and others and move on.

And here I thought I didn't have anything to say. Isn't that beautiful how that goes?

So today I'm going to hang out with some class material. I'm taking an online class to further develop my skill of being an online teacher. I know that shift is happening. I know about this wave. I know that people are waking up and they are seeking help. I try to come at things with the sense of hey – you already know. You might be unconscious to what you know, you might not know that you know but there's nothing that you don't know that I know that I'm going to give to you. You know what I'm saying?! This is just a really important thing for me. We all know what we need to know, but we've been so trained away from it that we think we don't know. This is what I've been going through these last 100 days, if not longer. I think that I don't have all that I need, that I don't know how. Turns out, I do. As you begin to unhook from the world of effects that keeps telling you it's outside of yourself and begin to tap into the messages that keep turning you back toward yourself, there's a shift.

I'm excited about having the time to put some things together that have been bubbling up inside of me. I imagine getting to Alaska might create a little bit of a space; though certainly, here with my mom, there's more than enough space too. So right away, there's my mind thinking that I don't have everything I need in this moment to do something and that I have to wait for conditions to change so I can have the perfect time, experience, or space. Isn't that fascinating? This is what happens when you meditate for an hour every day for 90 days. You may still say those things, but then you have an immediate awareness of what you just said and you think, *that's not true at all.* And why is that? Because I said so. Because I have an awakened awareness now.

Here's the thing. You still may be running around the wheel but at least you're aware of the wheel and you're aware of your running and there are these beautiful moments in which that awareness communicates an opportunity for you to change your thinking. As the great Ernest Holmes said, "Change your thinking, change your life."

Day 91: Problems are In Time. Solutions are Out of Time

I am so lit up right now. I knew there was a reason I didn't record my video right after meditation because there was something I had to experience that was important to share with you. I had a phone call and I didn't necessarily get triggered on the call, but I certainly got triggered after I hung up. I was getting upset, so I said, "Spirit, you need to help me out with this. I'm not quite sure why this is happening. I'd appreciate some sort of answer, guidance, or something."

I came upstairs to get ready to do my radio show and I remembered that I had forgotten to finish watching Michael Beckwith's Wednesday night live stream. So I put it on, and lo and behold, there was the answer. I am so grateful to Reverend Michael

Bernard Beckwith and what is being channeled through him right now.

His message was this: Problems and issues are in time. The answers and the solutions are in the eternal. The way that he taught that was by putting on some rocking music. What does he start with? The great tune, "September" by Earth, Wind, and Fire. Then he did one of his own songs. Each time he stopped the music just like musical chairs and he had us just be still, feeling the vibration and realizing that, in that moment, in that space and in that vibration, there are no problems. There are no issues! There are just the vibrations of solutions and the answers. It's something you have to experience. When I get up to Alaska, I'm going to do everything I can to bring these experiences to people. To have it inside your own body is where it's at.

I realized – wait a minute – I'm not here to be a daughter, friend, or sister. I'm here to be the vibration of love. I'm here right now. I can only speak about right now in my life. I'm here to be a healing presence. And let me tell you what is a priority for me. My number one priority is my feelings. My emotional life is my number one priority. Maintaining, sustaining, and activating joy, peace, love, abundance, gratitude, prosperity, clarity – that is my number one job. That creates the vibrational currency of my experience of my life and of life in general. When I am in that place, when I am dancing my ass off and enjoying it, that's all there is. This is why I love music so much. It is the vibration of the eternal and it activities the same within us and we become this vibrational match to joy. Music is a tonic and it heals the toxicity in our bodies.

Sometimes I have to have the old experience over and over again so that it gives me the opportunity to create a new experience. When you can string along enough new moments, you have a new experience. I'm grateful for all the people who pressed my buttons. I'm grateful for every moment in which I am being triggered, because it helps me see where, in my system, I still have something besides the vibration of love. And if

I'm here for any one reason, I'm here to dissolve and resolve anything that is unlike love. I'm here to dissolve and resolve any lies that I have been told or that I have told myself about who I am and why I am here.

So remember, it's the weekend. Turn up the music. Find the groove that makes you move. Share it with your parents, your family, your partners, your friends. Dance, dance, dance! Michael Beckwith also said that the cosmos is always celebrating and it's looking to localize the celebration within me and within you. Music and dance and chanting and walking in nature, yoga, all of these practices – prayer, meditation – all these things that we do give the cosmos a point for localizing that which is the universal celebration. The Universe is trying to make a point and it's using you. Bring it on!

Day 92: With Eight Days Left, I'm Happy to Say I'm not Confused. Oh, There May be Confusion but I'm not Confused.

The humidity was so intense that, when the rains finally came, I stayed outside and got deliciously soaking wet. Now the night sky is looking beautiful here in the great state of New Jersey. The clouds have been magnificent today.

Today I became the boy that my parents didn't have. Camillo was my grandpa's name and I was named Camille after him. My mom lives in this old world in which boys have to do all the heavy work and girls either shouldn't do it or can't do it. This includes everything from changing the fan blades, which she thought I had to get my nephew to do, to trimming the massive row of trees on the property. I was able to do that to the best of my ability, given my height and the height of the ladder. Though I did slice through a wire, unfortunately, which I have since repaired.

I'm humbled by the practice. Yesterday I was so fired up and I'm fine today. I'm grateful and I'm at peace right now. This is like going to the gym every day, an idea that's very familiar. I actually created a course called, "Strengthen your Spiritual

Muscles." I loved that. in just 45 minutes, an entire 4-part workshop came through me. In it I teach four spiritual practices: meditation, visioning, affirmative prayer, and circulation. What does it take to strengthen a muscle? For me, it takes work. It takes getting a weight and lifting it over and over and making your muscles burn and making that lactic acid run through your body the next day because it hurts so good. Spiritual muscles are strengthened through spiritual practices. It's the same thing.

I continue to simply be grateful for these 92 days. I realized that I came into this messed up, man. I was spinning like a spinning top, and here I am – 92 days later – and I'm not. And when I feel confused, I know that I'm not confused; rather, there's confusion. And even though I don't have the answers to everything and I'm going to Alaska next week and I have mixed feelings about how that will work out, BUT I'm not confused.

I thought I was going to be able to stay with a friend, but that's not going to work out. I'm not panicking because all of my needs are met and there's always someone that helps out. I'm lifting my sights from basic things like lodging and cars to thinking about what I want to share when I get up there. I think I'd like to do an event at my spiritual center as a template, a blueprint, a dress rehearsal, for something larger.

The future is ripe with potential, like the air tonight. Right before the clouds opened and the rain came, the air was pregnant. It was so feminine. It reminded me of how I used to feel right before my menstrual cycle, so full. It reminds me of how it feels right before an orgasm, something so beautiful and seeded and fertile. Then the clouds just opened and there was this profound release. We need the feminine. It's just so interesting to be in a time where apparent leaders of my country have no hesitation to mock and berate women, the feminine. But the feminine is rising. We need to rise to balance the patriarchal way that's collapsing. The matriarchal way must step into the mix and balance out the patriarchal way.

Day 93: Vacation

There is no video for Day 93. Though I did my meditation, I didn't roll tape right away and then never got to it. More truthfully, I chose not to do it. Instead I decided to let a picture tell the day's story.

Day 94: Emotional Rescue

I was talking to a friend the other day and having a very human moment. He said something like, "Well if I was meditating for 91 days, I certainly wouldn't be having this kind of an issue." It wasn't that harsh, but I got a little defensive and said whatever I said. I have been incredibly emotional today. I'm not sure if it's important to know the Why, though when something lasts as long as it has today, the mind wants an answer. It wants a justification. It wants to know why. *Why am I so upset? Why am I crying? Why this and why that?* I could say it's because I'm leaving on Friday. My heart is very full around leaving my mom and my sister, Janice.

It's about other things too, like going to Alaska and not knowing where I'm going to stay. I don't have a place and I have to figure that out or do I? But I guess my point is that life happens. The heart feels. This is not about, "Oh, I'm on Day 94 and I shouldn't feel anything." This is more like, "I'm on Day 94 and I feel everything. I've allowed myself to do that." I haven't had a drop of alcohol, or anything else, for that matter, in over a month. Today was really the first day when I thought, *If I had a drink or something else, it would take the edge off of my emotions.* Not that there would be anything wrong if I chose that because, as an adult, it's a conscious choice. I don't have a problem with that. I don't have a problem with alcohol. Something else is going on. But in that moment, I had a real understanding of why, sometimes, I've reached for those things and why, sometimes, we reach for those things to take the edge off of being sad and upset for an entire day. We don't want to feel that anymore.

But if 94 days of meditation has showed me one thing, it's that feeling is where it's at. Whether it's joy or sadness, feeling is where it's at. And even though I may not want to feel it, feeling it is the best gift I could give myself. And being honest with people around me about what I'm going through is the best gift I can give all of us. The gift is to feel. Life is precious! Our time here is finite, though we are infinite beings. Meanwhile, I wonder, man – do I need to bite the bullet here and make a decision? Do I need to go to Alaska and wrap things up in a way that brings me back here until she passes, however far away that might be? It's very heavy on my heart.

So it's 8:00 pm and I avoided doing this all day today. Though I have no problem feeling what I feel, it's still a little vulnerable feeling in front of a camera and then posting it on freakin' Facebook. Today I'm grateful for my family, I'm grateful for my mom, and I'm grateful for the many blessings I have. I'm confident now because I have clarity and I know the One who's thinking through me has clarity, that whatever answers I seek are on their way to me if I don't already have them.

Six more days of this incredible, life-changing, transformative experiment. It blows my mind what these 96 days have been all about. It's just something else. May I have the courage and focus to finish writing about it.

Day 95: Say Goodbye, It's Independence Day

This is Day 95 on the Fourth of July! I think of that Bruce Springsteen song, "Independence Day" in which he sings, *Say goodbye, it's Independence Day*. What was he talking about in that song? He had to say goodbye to his father, his family, his boyhood, and step into his manhood. He had to say goodbye because it was his Independence Day. I wish you Independence

– freedom from anger, from hate, from anything that doesn't light you up – all the low vibrational stuff. May we just do whatever we need to do every day, every hour, every minute, every second of the day to keep our spirits and vibrations high and, when they're not, wrap our arms around ourselves and hug ourselves tightly with all the love we can. And when we can't do it ourselves, may we reach out for help and never allow ourselves to keep going when the tank is empty.

I learned how to keep going when the tank is empty, but guess what happens when I do that? I get stressed and my fuse is non-existent and I snap and yell and do all those things that are nothing I ever want to do. But I let myself run empty, and then I allow myself to keep going, as if what I was doing was more important than refueling. Why is that? I don't know. Clearly I'm still strengthening my ability to not do that anymore. It happens a lot here in New Jersey. My sister pointed out tonight that, unless it's an emergency, I should keep my focus on what I need to do for myself. It turns out that I do have a large pile of things because I haven't put my attention on myself in quite a few days.

And now with just a few days left – oh boy – I feel a lot of stress and pressure. But since I've been feeling that way for quite a few days now, I'm going to try to do something different tonight. Because, you know, it's the Fourth of July, and this is Day 95.

Day 96: On a Hot Summer Night

Today I had a chance to connect with the Flow Group online. Kyle Cease was able to join us tonight, and it was a wonderful experience. It was a joy to see my friends again, and to see Kyle, and to have him ask about how it's been, and to be able to tell him I'm on Day 96 and to share with him some of the insights I've had. It was lovely to see his response to what I was saying. Things got very exciting. It's like, while I'm over here looking at what I think isn't happening, the Universe is planning something so magnificent and so much bigger than anything my mind can conceive. When I see it and I have glimpses of what's coming and it's presented to me in flashes of insight, I just go – oh my gosh.

It helps me see more clearly how the mind's job is multipurpose. One of the things the mind is here to do is to keep the familiar active. The mind does not like it when something new emerges out of something that's not yet been, because it feels threatened. Things are falling away in a big and sometimes scary way, but what rushes in is so much bigger. I told Kyle about revisiting the video that I made when I was applying for the Flow Group weekend, where I said the two things that have been fueling this trip: I wanted to live from my heart all the time, and I wanted to make room for the gifts within me that were seeking to be released.

I knew those were big things at the time, but I also had no comprehension of what command I was giving the Universe and what command I was giving my soul. In order to live from the heart, you have to deconstruct the mind's role in your life. And when we ask, "What is within me that's yet to emerge?", everything that has been previously active has to, if not fall away, be on pause so that there's room for the new to emerge.

I got a text from a friend I hadn't spoken with in a while and she asked me, "How are you doing?" I wrote back and said, "I don't think I can answer that in a text." But I've been thinking about that. How am I doing? If the mind answers that, holy Toledo, sit down for the story it's going to tell. If you were to ask my heart how I'm tracking, the heart would say – "Fantastic! Everything is spot on and right on schedule as it should be." I love that it has this perspective, even though my mind has a different story about where I am.

I really had a bad moment today, trying to introduce a way to give my mom some of these wonderful supplements for her knee, and she couldn't grasp it. Instead of just stopping and getting out of the situation, I stayed. That was a bad thing to do. It felt like my head was in a vice grip. The daughter in me just lost it while witnessing her mom not being able to do something that she's always been able to do. Thank god and goddess that I can go back to my mother and apologize and ask for forgiveness. I can't be the only person or caregiver that has moments of shame when their behavior is less than loving. I don't know what's to come of all of this, if this is something I need to write about, talk about, have a support group or go to a support group! I know I need some help to process what I'm going through.

I ended the night with prayer, and I'm calmer. I'm tired. What-ever happened is what happened, so I guess it was supposed to happen exactly as it did. Spirit is either everywhere or nowhere. God or Love - whatever the word you use - is either everywhere present, or nowhere at all. I will keep going, but I'm ready to have a break from the tears, that's for sure. I feel like I could use a week on a beach. But for right now, I'm going to settle for a good night's sleep.

Day 97: No One and No Thing Outside of You is Your Source

I came into my meditation this morning with this thing about leaving Sunday instead of tomorrow, Friday, for Alaska. I was aware of the typical angst that comes from my mind presenting this to me as, *What should I do? I don't know what to do.* It is very important to notice how the questions create the emotion. It has nothing to do with, "I don't know what to do." It has nothing to do with, "What should I do?" It simply has to do with, "What does my heart need?"

For the most part, I've been living from the mind with many moments of living from the heart. However, after seeing how my mind works and how its filters work and what my mind can do based on those filters and agenda, I much prefer to bear witness to it, but not follow it all the time especially when my heart is not in alignment with what the mind is saying.

Back behind my mind is The Mind, and most times the heart

and that Mind are in alignment. I came into this meditation with the awareness that I simply wanted to be available for what my heart was needing and to go toward what felt light, knowing that it was going to cost money to change my ticket. Money is never not part of the equation. And my relationship to that money, at least in the world of effects, has not changed so far. To make that be the deciding factor is not what this is about, either. So I went into the meditation asking my heart to reveal to me what it needed. I'm going to use the words feminine and masculine, not male and female. This is not about genders or people, it's about archetypes.

My experience is that, when my needs are feminine, those needs are dismissed. When my needs are masculine needs, they tend to drive the decision. So the masculine needs sound like, *You've got to do it. You already paid for the ticket and it's going to cost more money. Just get it together.* All of that stuff comes from my mind. The feminine needs come from my heart. The feminine needs are, *I need more time. I want to feel differently than how I do right now.* The masculine needs say, *Feel however you need to feel, and get on the plane tomorrow, anyway.* One is loving, one is harsh.

My point is, I'm here to not dismiss my needs. I know what I need. I know what I feel inside. Too often we dismiss what we need because we're measuring it against something else that's telling us what our needs should be. I'm not here to do that anymore. I decided I was going to change that plane ticket to Sunday when I came out of my meditation. The relief that I felt because of that decision was powerful. It's not because I'm trying to delay leaving my mom; it has nothing to do with my mom. It has to do with asking my heart what I need and being willing to give myself that.

I'm also looking at going back to Alaska with an awareness of how different I feel, how I've changed, and feeling like I'm going back in a new way, having a new relationship with all that I've been there. I'm going back with this renewed awareness. OK. Let's go feel into who I've been and what I've been doing and see how it feels, and to go toward what excites me. I'm not going back to feel like I have to go towards the familiar, the things I've already done, because now I know that that's the mind's agenda. What's already known is from the past. The mind does not like how the heart is, being in the moment and being available to infinite possibilities and trusting that everything is working out for my highest good. I'm not dismissing the need for goals and all of that; let's not take it to the extreme. I'm simply pointing out that my mind is freaking out because I have not allowed it to put me into things that it already knows from last year simply because that would fill the space of me having something to do.

Today is Day 97, and I'm looking forward to putting the oxygen mask on myself and to significantly reducing the stimuli that has been active in my life. I'm looking forward to being quiet and still, to gather up what I need to gather up to come back to the center of who I am so that I can prepare myself for the journey ahead. I'm looking forward to honoring who I am and what I need, no matter what it looks like, no matter what my mind has to say about it, and no matter what anybody else has to say about it. If I don't bring those needs to myself, who's going to? Of course, the Spirit is, because all of my needs are met by It. But you know what I'm saying. This is about me understanding and learning to ask, "What are my needs? What are those real needs?" And then to bring them to myself.

Day 98: The Training Wheels are Off!

I've been stressed about my housing when I return to Alaska because my mind has been telling me that it's supposed to happen a specific way and since it's not, nothing is happening. Of course, to the Universe, everything is always happening all the time. To the Universe, it's impossible to think that nothing is happening.

So I'm very cognizant and aware, now, that my mind is presenting neutral data to me through its own filter, and it's often as if something is against me or not working out for me. It's trying to present this whole lodging thing like, *What's going on? Maybe you need to reconsider all this. Maybe this experiment of going back and forth should be over.* Even when a friend of mine said I could stay at their place, my mind was like, *Well it's not this house or that house or what we really want.* Even though my needs were met, the ego mind said it wasn't enough!

I actually own a house in Anchorage, one that I've been lending to friends since I left. I texted them to say, "I'm coming into town as planned and I'm looking forward to checking in with you guys." They texted back with, "OK, but we won't be back in town until July 26th. We gave the key to the neighbor and they're going to water the plants." My body lit up and I said, "Any chance you want a house sitter?" As it turns out, they do.

So when I fly into Anchorage, I'm going home, literally! I'm going back to my own home as my first housesitting gig. While my mind was trying to convince me that nothing was happening, the Universe was plotting for my good. The Universe was putting together the highest possible outcome, and that's being in my own home! I have a calmness about me now, because I know without a shadow of a doubt that this Thing has got it going on. This Thing is awake, aware, and alive. This Thing that breathes me also knows me. It's here with me. It knows all that I desire because it's moving through me as these desires, and It's got everything figured out. Whatever intelligence that was able to put that together is putting everything else together. So, even though I go back to Alaska with things looking differently and feeling differently and the ways in which I express myself not necessarily obvious to me, I'm OK. Something fantastic is being rolled out. All I have to do is maintain my vibrational frequency to be a match for the highest desires of my life.

Day 99: Forget the Laundry List, Just Do It

Ninety Nine days! It makes me want to sing: *99 bottles of beer on the wall, 99 bottles of beer!* Ninety-nine days of meditating for an hour every day and rolling tape. Ninety-nine days of not wanting to roll tape because I prefer the microphone. Ninety-nine days of rolling tape however I looked, and boy, were there some looks, and loving what I saw. Ninety-nine days of being authentic and real, no matter the tears that flowed and the heart that burst open, no matter the words that came out of my mouth. Ninety-nine days of just showing up and sharing who I am with you. Ninety-nine days of insights, ninety-nine days of awareness and observations and bringing quite a bit up to the light. In my awareness, things have dissolved.

And yet, there's more. I'm going to continue to meditate. That's part of my life now. I'm going to take a break from rolling tape for sure because I want to do some writing and other things around this content. However, it's really important for me to be clear about what I need to do to be happy. I come from an Italian Catholic background, and there are a lot of ancestral patterns and beliefs that come with my lineage. Much of them came out of survival and fear, and I have become very clear that I do not want to continue any patterns that come out of survival and fear. I love them, however, that was a long time ago and things have changed. I'm taking a very close look at my ancestral patterns, and I'm simply releasing myself from them. I no longer need to carry them in my life. There is a lot of heaviness that comes through my family's lineage.

But you know what? I want to do something different. I might have to make some radical changes in my life, with life, to create the environment in which I am going to thrive internally. I want to create an internal environment mentally, emotionally, physically, and spiritually that gives me a leg up into thriving. The big thing is learning, this time around, that I am no longer here to manage any other relationship but my own to myself. I've gone back and I've gotten the little Camille, and she no longer has the assignment of emotionally managing others. She is not here to manipulate or control outcomes to create or maintain peace and harmony in the family. This is so big for me. I have really had to let go and grieve expectations and needs that have come out of my past that no longer serve me. I want to be free. I want to love people, but I don't want to maintain outcomes and the outer world of effects because of some pattern from the past. This is another powerful shift.

It's one idea to manipulate outcomes for peace and harmony; it's something else to show up AS peace and harmony.

This is about strengthening my spiritual muscles, strengthening these skills, strengthening this new awareness, and continuing to master this. I simply want to have happy, joyful, light, lively and lovely relationships. And yes, when it comes to family there will always be moments, but I want less of those moments. And it's not about how other people show up. It's all about me. It's about how I'm showing up and about what I'm still carrying. I've been mentioning my family but it has nothing to do with them; it has to do with me. There's only one thing happening and it's happening in, through, around, and as me. I'm still going through some radical transformation, that's for sure.

The other thing is, it's time to take a leap. Kyle said, "If you keep thinking about things, doing an event or writing the book, it becomes a mental addiction." I don't want mental addictions. I want to leap and I want to do. So what do I need to do next to take a leap? Do I need to rent a hall? Do I need to create an event? Maybe all of the above? I'm excited about going up to Alaska and making a leap. Today in my meditation something powerful came through, and maybe it's just a reworking of what already exists. I'm just going to start doing things.

My passion is the radio. My passion is the microphone and connection and transformation. These are the things I love doing. I'm spontaneous and I'm funny, too. How am I to package this in such a way that's fresh for me and for you? Something original. I'm original and so are you. All we have to do is keep showing up and giving ourselves permission to take our foot off the brakes and to live our lives fully, and we're on a roll.

I absolutely have some anxiety about leaving tomorrow. I'm tired, and I've overdone it once again. It takes a lot of work to clean and prepare things for me to leave my mom. Interestingly, my mother said, "I didn't tell you to do those things," which is true, but I did them anyway. I have to look at why I'm so comfortable exhausting myself for another person. That's something I learned growing up, too. Give until you're empty for another person. It may have come out of the past, but I don't want to exhaust myself for another person anymore, even my mom. My mom is right; she didn't ask me to do those things, but I did and I exhausted myself.

So I'm keeping it light today. I want to be the expression of love in this last day and a half. Maybe I just need to enjoy the day and enjoy those who are around me, and keep my heart open and ready. As Bruce Springsteen sings, "It takes a leap of faith to get things going. In your heart you must trust."

Day 100: I DID IT!!

This is Day 100, and it's no surprise that this falls on the day I go to the airport. I can remember when I first started; the 100th day seemed like an eternity. In a way, it was and it has been, because the person that started this experiment 100 days ago is not necessarily the same person that I am today. I am just kind of in awe of what exactly this whole thing has been about and the changes that I've gone through and I'm going through still.

One thing's for sure, though: if I'm going to have a new way of living, that means I have to have a new way of responding to the old way of living. I have to see each moment as a pause, right? When things happen, when I feel upset or the triggers happen, my old way would be to allow emotion to take me. The old way would be to become upset, to let the tears flow, but what I'm realizing today is that to have a new way of living, I have to have a new way of responding to life. This is a real strengthener for me. It's about overcoming and changing a life-long pattern. I know I can do it. There are ample opportunities being presented to me to do it. I have to remain mindful and conscious of emotional upset that I believe others are causing and to love myself and cut other people some slack.

I want to thank you, also, for being a part of this journey. I had no idea what the hell was going on most of the time. It's really only in this last lap that things have become somewhat clear to me, and I guess The Confusion Experiment has proven itself to be a success. As I said the other day, though there is confusion, I'm not necessarily confused.

I'm definitely experiencing a tender heart leaving my mom. It's difficult knowing that her car is in the driveway and she's not able to drive it right now and she doesn't understand why. We'll see what happens with us in the future. I'm going back to Alaska with my feet on the ground, ready to rock 'n roll. It's a time for action, it's a time for leaps, it's a time to roll down the road without training wheels. Day 100, and I'm ready to board the plane to Portland and then on to Anchorage. I'm ready to take flight.

Love to you and to your family and yourself. Love to me, love to my mom and my family, and happy trails.

The Findings

Journey to the Center of the Mind

Congratulations! You have completed The Confusion Experiment, a 100 day journey from the head to the heart and beyond. My hope is that you are inspired and encouraged to do your own experiment, to discover what is true for you, to explore how it is that your mind works, to examine what your thinking is presenting to you and to begin to question anything that doesn't light you up.

The point of any experiment is to share the findings, so I offer you these nuggets of insight because, even though this was a personal experience, the information I received is universal. These revelations offer a practical education that you can apply to your everyday living, which in turn can lead you into a deepening of your own life experience. This information came from the notes I took after my weekends with Kyle Cease and Michael Beckwith, and my own inspired writings after watching all 100 videos.

Here's what I learned:

Meditation is really the honing of the skill to be still. Meditation is about the practice of sitting with yourself, which is actually very difficult for most people to do because we're not comfortable being with ourselves. We're also very addicted to stimulation, and the idea of having none for an hour - let alone 15 minutes - is terrifying for most people. We've also convinced ourselves that we don't have the time. That's why meditation is a practice. By doing it every day, you strengthen your meditation muscle and become more comfortable simply being with yourself.

Meditation is not about stopping your thoughts. For those who think meditation is about stopping your thoughts, I would say that the majority of my time meditating is filled with thoughts. What changed is my relationship to them.

Meditation is not about the elimination of your thoughts. It can't be and here's why. The mind's job is to think. It's like a manufacturing warehouse, churning out thoughts all day and all night. When we go to sleep, the mind is still creating thoughts - your thoughts, my thoughts, everybody's thoughts. I believe they swirl around at night while we're asleep, waiting. Then when you wake up – sometimes before you even open your eyes – they come rushing in! Thoughts, thoughts and more thoughts! So meditation is NOT about stopping thoughts. They're here to stay. Also, meditation is very quick with the impact it has on the body. Though I left Kyle's retreat and returned to Anchorage feeling very depressed, by Day 8 of my experiment I was feeling better. My mind was still blown to pieces, but I noted in that video that I felt better.

There is no method of meditation. Not to say that there aren't different teachings that are valid and worthwhile, because I too teach different "types" of meditation. However, I now believe that there is no necessary method. If you think there's a method, that delays the experience. "I have to go find the method because I don't know what it is. Somebody has to teach me." No.

The method of meditation is, get a chair. Sit down. Set the timer on your phone for 60 minutes (or 6). Close your eyes. Get the popcorn and watch the show. That's it. And the next day, do it again. Then, when you find yourself attached to your thoughts and suddenly you're shopping in Costco or having an imaginary conversation with someone in your head, come back to the breath. Always come back to the breath.

Did you know that the breath is the only thing that can interrupt the autonomic nervous system? Do you know that we're wired for 'fight or flight' and the breath is the only thing that tells the brain it's not in crisis? Do you know that when you take a deep breath you just communicated to your mind that everything's OK?

For example, when you get a message from your boss or your friend that says, "We need to talk," your brain goes into its 'fight or flight' response. If you take a conscious breath, you're telling your mind, "There's no charging elephant!" This is so important because the breath halts the secretion of adrenaline and cortisol, hormones that were never meant to run non-stop in your body. They were designed to serve your system in short term doses in that small window of "fight or flight". Now however, we're so overstimulated that everything is perceived as a threat and the constant secretion of these hormones is depleting our immune system. This is why they say, "Stress kills." So, breathe.

Meditation reveals the One behind the thoughts. Whatever the word is for you – Universe, God, Allah, Higher Power, The Thing Itself, there's a You behind the you. There's a Mind behind your mind and thank goodness for that! This is the Mind that knows all because It is All. I like to call It "the Intelligence that holds all the planets in place." This is the Mind that communicates via our intuition. It knows stuff and wants to share! Meditation connects you with this Mind and the benefits are life changing. Get to know this Mind as quickly as possible because it's awesome.

Meditation shows you things (though maybe not when you think it will). Some amazing things happened while I meditated - the lava lamp stuff, the tingling sensation in my head, feeling like I was snatched out of time and space - but so much more happened afterwards. My morning hour of meditation gave me realizations throughout the rest of the day, no matter what I was doing. Answers came quickly. Lost items were found easily. Things flowed without my effort. And the insights I had around personal growth issues that had been plaguing me for years popped up in my conscious mind as nuggets of perspective and insight that caused one healing after another.

We are not our thoughts. For many weeks in the beginning of this experiment, I was tumbling and twisting and rolling inside a tornado of my thoughts. "I am confused. I am sad. I am unhappy." I believed I was those thoughts. I identified myself with them, as them.

After several weeks of meditation, I felt like I was sucked out of that whirlwind and put right on the edge of it. I still felt the pull into this crazy vortex of thoughts, but I started to question – wait a minute. AM I confused? AM I confusion?

Then after a while, I moved far enough away from the chaos that I was able to observe my thoughts. It was similar to sitting in a movie theater. What a shit show! No wonder I've been confused and depressed. Look at this thing! It's crazy, it's insanity....and I love it. Because it's mine. That's when I realized that I am not my thoughts, I am something else. Over time, I found myself sitting with the Me behind the me, the Divine One, seeing things from Its perspective. That's when I realized this is the Intelligence that breathes me, that beats my heart and it has nothing to do with the mind that wants to see how many people liked my post on Facebook!

It's important to learn how to look at things, because the mind loves to present life to us through its own filters and those filters are usually distorted. Meditation allowed me to distance myself far enough away from my thinking that I finally understood that there may be confusion, but I am not confused. Truly a transformational moment.

The mind needs to know. We have an obsession with knowing. Vision boards, goals, five-year plans, day planners, time management, to-do lists, all so that you know what you're doing, where you're going, and how you'll get there. This obsession with knowing places a high value on the mind, so much so that I can now see that sometimes when I thought I was using my mind, my mind was really using me.

In addition, the mind doesn't like the way the heart works. The mind wants to determine a new moment based on what's already familiar, using the past as its reference point to how it ought to be... except a new moment has no past. The heart replaces facts and evidence with feelings and uses its own set of qualifiers called intuition and instinct. These two inherent qualities have very little value in our society's formula for success and that is particularly true when you experience change. So, when you take a leap of faith, you don't necessarily have all the information. That's intentional. Life loves to play.

But because the mind needs to know everything before it leaps - past attempts, failures and risks, likelihood of success - it rarely gives the green light. This is why we often feel so stuck and unable to move forward or make a decision. Meanwhile, the heart uses feelings as a preview. Now I can appreciate the importance of Kyle's question, "How do you feel?" This is the tug of war between the heart and the mind that was so keenly represented in the "left side/right side of the page" exercise.

In addition, because the mind works with what it knows, it has specific filters about how things should look and, if it doesn't look like that, then it must mean "nothing is happening." I suffered from this time and time again and was able to see that it was a cause of not just stress but depression as I got stuck in the belief that nothing was happening while so much was. Another major breakthrough. The mind can take neutral data and create a conclusion that isn't true. This is why it's critical to challenge what your mind presents to you. In doing that myself, I realized I was trying to build my future from the past.

The heart is more like a GPS. A GPS doesn't give you every direction all at once before you leave the driveway; you'd never get anywhere. Once you identify where it is you want to go, the GPS figures out the "how" and tells you one direction at a time and you trust it to get you where you've told it you want to go.

That's exactly how the heart works. The instructions from the heart come after you leap through instinct and intuition, the GPS of the heart. If your heart is telling you to do something, believe that it's important and knows the way!

The heart goes by feelings. I'll give you an example. I have really strong instincts; I'm sure you do, too. Throughout my spiritual journey, using my practices and tools, my intuition has gotten sharper. So when I left Alaska in 2013 and left my home, my career and my life behind, I knew I was ready for something else, something more, something that would take all the different aspects of who I was and bring them together, unified. I didn't know what it was I was ready for, but I had a feeling it would find me and I would recognize it. I trusted my instinct enough to take the leap of faith.

As I traveled into new territory, I can see now that when my instinct kicked in, my mind jumped in right after it and shouted, "Wait! You can't do that. That can't be right. We've never done this before. I can't look to the past and see how this has happened or worked out. We don't have a reference point. You can't possibly know! We should find someone who does." That well-presented, unexamined argument created doubt, that doubt caused me to not trust my instinct and that caused separation to my own knowing self as I believed the outer world knew more than my inner world.

So I went outside of myself for the tiniest things like picking a logo for my website. My first choice was a blue lotus but what do I know about a good logo for a website? I better find the people who do know. I asked all my friends and business colleagues for their feedback. Of course, everyone had a different opinion! Now I have way too much information. I'm overwhelmed, confused, and paralyzed. I don't know which way to go. Meanwhile, weeks have gone by until finally I say to myself, "Pick the blue one!" In the end, I came back to the first logo that I loved because of how it made me feel, but the distance that was driven between me and my knowing self was miles wide and the time spent second guessing myself caused incredible stress. So did my need for perfectionism.

The moral of this story is I knew what was right for me from the beginning because of how I felt when I saw it: my heart loved that blue logo. The mind can only work with what it knows. The heart works with what it feels.

The mind has taken us collectively as far as we can go. Do you know what I'm saying? We're seeing it in our everyday living. The mind has run its course as the tool for our evolution. It's not the mind that's going to take us to the next place. It's the heart. That's why I'm so excited that you're here and you're reading this. This is about you making the choice to open your heart a little bit more today, tonight and tomorrow. It's about listening to your heart, getting familiar with its language and trusting its guidance.

Here's why that's important. We've effectively cut the heart out of the equation as well as the value that instinct and intuition bring in balancing how we know. Instead, our model of success is what you know and who you know. Knowing, that's success, and knowing leads to clarity, another seemingly important piece to happiness. You already know how I feel about clarity! No wonder I felt like I was a failure in these last three years. I can see this so clearly now. I thought I didn't know but really, I didn't know that I knew! Now, I know that I know. That doesn't mean that I'm not going to take a course and learn something from someone else. However, my new method is to first turn within and ask. That process acknowledges that there is something beyond my own thinking mind that knows, and I can communicate with It, and It with me. We are the guru we've been looking for.

We've trained to look outside of ourselves. We actually believe that people and things are our source. We've come to believe that it's someone else's job to satisfy our needs and that always leads to disappointment because it's built on a false premise that your source is external. For too long we've believed that the outer world creates the inner world, so we need people to be a certain way and say certain things to make us feel certain ways.

I have actually believed that people make me feel different emotions, and if only they would say something else or if only they had done something else, then I would feel differently. That has failed pretty consistently throughout the majority of my adult life. It's called control; it's called manipulation; it's called insanity. But this is what we do! We believe people are causing our inner world, our emotions, how we feel. We believe that they need to change before we do. I've finally realized – nope – I'm responsible. It's going on inside me, it's mine to own and work with. As the great Reverend Rainbow Johnson said long ago, "I may have pressed your buttons, but I didn't install them." I've never forgotten that saying. It's a good one to remember.

We're afraid to feel. We're so afraid to feel that we'd rather blame others for our feelings. We've been told to numb them, avoid them, project them, to do all kinds of things instead of feeling them. But let me tell you, what's real is that we feel. Clearing stuck energy by giving ourselves permission to feel all the hurt, the anger, the disappointment and everything else that has become, as Eckhart Tolle calls it, a "pain body" is critical to being able to live from our hearts. If your heart is clogged up with unforgiveness, how can your best self emerge? If you're riddled with shame and blame, how can you trust yourself to leap? My mind was always showing me how someone else was to blame. Meditation showed me what was mine. Another game changer.

It's time we mature and own our feelings. How do you do that? By learning how to sit with your feelings and feel them, by allowing yourself to become comfortable with your own discomfort. That's the skill to develop and meditation is one way to do it.

We've got to do the "turnaround." We have to turn away from the world of effects, the headlines, what doesn't feed us and what makes us heavy, and turn towards what makes us feel better. Here's what I've learned – life is mostly a vibrational thing and it's pretty awesome. We're here to feel good. When I look at the headlines, I don't feel good. So, what am I going to do? Am I going to take my precious, creative, never-been-here-before moment and react to something that's already done? How does my emotional reaction change a headline? Better to ask, "What's mine to do?" and put your creative energy towards being a solution versus a reaction.

One of the things I learned in meditation is that I want to be right on the edge of the problem. If I'm in the problem, I can't be a place for the solution to come through me. I can't be the solution if I'm in the problem. I want to see the problem but not necessarily be absorbed by it or taken down by it. This is the new place for us to be: outside of the problem just enough to understand it, to ride the edge of what's happening so as to be a vessel through which a solution can come.

Yes, these things that are happening in our world hurt. It's crazy the depth of poverty, oppression and violence that fills our lives. But crazy is not going to fix crazy. Love will fix it. The heart will fix it. Peace will fix it. Harmony will fix it. You're not going to get your answers from "out there." You'll get it from inside you, from your heart, from the One that knows.

Be willing to change. One of the things that happened along the way was that I had to say goodbye to me. As I have been moving through this time of reorganization, I never did so without bringing my radio personality into the mix. I can see now that this was another time in which I spoke about myself in the third person. Meditation revealed to me I had been fighting for "her" place in my new life. It wasn't until I came back to Anchorage in the summer of 2017 that I understood what was happening.

I was doing some fill-in work at KNBA radio. It was the first time back at my old stomping grounds since 2016 when I also did some part-time work while in town. With the headphones on, a song playing in my ears, I heard a voice say: "This is too limiting. You love music, but it's too limiting." I immediately thought, *You can't take this from me*. But then I realized that nobody was taking anything from me. It was all going with me, but it was going to convert its form and its shape into something new. Wasn't this what I asked for? To let the new emerge?

This openness to change was a huge turning point for me. I had been trying all this time to force who I'd been in radio, this great rock n roll DJ, into a new idea that was not yet fully formed. I can see why I was so attached to this identity; it's who I've known myself to be for a long time, so the idea of letting that go was terrifying. Who would I be if I wasn't that? In that instant, the butterfly began to flap her wings.

Who we believe ourselves to be, how we see ourselves, the identities we have, the roles we play.... when you deepen your awareness of the Self, when you consciously and actively co-create your own evolution, shift happens! Things fall away, you outgrow relationships and jobs, sometimes you even outgrow you. The more I changed internally the more my outer world fell away. The old skin cannot hold the new wine.

There's a new measurement of success. Another construct I had to let go of was how I measured success. In radio, success is measured by the size of the audience. It is so important that the hour is divided into quarter hour measurements. The radio station with the biggest audience won and the DJ with the most listeners won and that made the sales people win because then they could raise their prices and make more money. The quintessential ripple effect so the pressure to be #1 was pretty intense.

I didn't realize how influential this deeply seeded training was in my current life until I had a realization in the summer of 2017, after I had officially finished my 100 days of meditation (though I continued the practice after I was "done"). In August I created an event where I talked about The Confusion Experiment at the Alaska Center for Spiritual Living in Anchorage. The day before the event I was terribly anxious. I've learned that when I ask my inner Wise One a question It answers me, so I asked, "What is going on here? Why am I freaking out?" I realized that my mind was taking that audience-size measurement of success from so long ago and laying it over this new experience. It was doing exactly what it was supposed to do and that's exactly when I realized that measurement was no longer valid. I understood where it was coming from and why it was active; however, I also realized that I wasn't there to measure the success of my talk based on how many people were in the seats. Was I affirming a full house? Of course, but my awareness of what was causing my anxiety allowed me to unwrap myself from it. I was then able to redefine my success as something internal - the expansion of my consciousness and the opening of my heart.

I also decided to redefine what success meant and declared I was already successful simply because I was doing it! It was the first Facebook Live event I'd ever done, and I was ecstatic that I was willing to be so out of my comfort zone. It was a huge learning curve for me and just having that work was such a success. I had over 124 views while live and to this day over 500 people have watched that 52-minute video. As soon as I released the audience, it showed up.

The New Design for Living. The world as we know it is collapsing. It's part of our natural evolution and necessary for what is coming. However, for many it's terrifying. We're here inside this time of massive change and people are freaking out. We're turning around and saying to each other, "Who's got the instructions? I'm getting fired, this is ending, this is happening; how do I do this? Somebody give me the instructions!"

The problem with the old way is that it doesn't give you the instructions for the new way because the old way doesn't even know it's dying. Besides, it couldn't give you the right instructions for the new way even if it wanted to because it doesn't have them. The new infrastructure is being built from the inside out. The new design for living is within us. We have everything we need.

Life can be easy. Life does not have to be hard. That's the old way of living. The old way is, you have to be exhausted by the end of your day to know you put in a good day. Why would we want to exhaust ourselves as a measurement that it was a good, productive, successful day? It's killing us! Have you noticed? Our tanks are empty.

With this new way emerging through us and as us, we can find ourselves standing on a solid foundation as change brings the walls tumbling down. That's the conscious evolutionary moment before us: to realize that the only real world is the one within, and it wants out. This world can never be touched, affected, changed, or diminished by the external world of effects. Meditation takes you to that place and helps you realize through personal experience that 99.9 percent of what is real is unseen, including ourselves.

Epilogue

When I did the submission video for Kyle, I made two life changing statements: 1) I want to live from my heart all the time and 2) I want to release the gifts and talents that lay dormant within me. I unleashed those two commands to the Universe unaware of how they would manifest and what I would have to let go of to get exactly what I wanted. Turns out, I had to go through the deconstruction of my mind so I could live fully from my heart, and meditation was the way. I didn't understand that until many weeks into the experiment, but once I did, it was an intense realization. As far as unborn gifts and talents, I'd say "author" is a good start.

This experiment showed me that to truly be alive meant that I had to surrender everything I had been taught about living, and that's a huge request. On top of that, I had to go deep inside of myself and release the part of me that identified with that formula for living. Also a huge request. My transformation asked me to unlearn the value of knowledge and relearn the value of feelings. It also asked that I let go of the me that had gotten me this far so I could meet the me that was taking me forward! I had to die to myself, like the caterpillar, so that the butterfly could be born. I had to amputate myself from comfortable habits, ways of being, patterns of behavior to stretch into the sometimes-painful discomfort of change. I had to journey to the center of my mind to find the key that unlocked the treasures of my heart.

My 100 day meditation experiment has gone on to become a way of life. The opportunities to put my awareness into practice continue, and so do the chances to love, trust, and care for myself as I navigate through my life and all that it is...which sometimes includes a lot of challenges. This leads me to the last finding of my experiment: Enlightenment isn't about the shit not hitting the fan; you just clean it up faster.

As I thought about how to end this book, I realized you can't end something that has no ending. And so, though this book is ending, the experiment continues because it's really good to be awake. Awake is where it's at. When I first began to wake up years ago, there were times I wanted to stuff myself back into the bottle of unconscious living because once you see, you can't un-see, and I wasn't ready to see all that was really true. To do so required a depth of letting go that I wasn't ready for. But I'm ready now and I wouldn't go back for anything in the world. I'm finally home. Besides, these wings have other plans.